Little Buddha Book Five

Little Buddha Book Five

Little Buddha
Book Five

Rob H. Geyer

Little Buddha Book Five

Little Buddha Book Five

ISBN-10: 8856691978

ISBN-13: 979-8856691978

Cover Image developed by Cheri Warren & Rob H
Geyer using Midjourney AI.

Little Buddha Book Five

Dedication

To all of those who have fallen in love with Claire,
Sam, Janine, and all of the other characters of the
Little Buddha book series, especially my Spiritual
Mastermind friends; Cheri and Dottie and my Little
Buddha Book Study friends.

Little Buddha Book Five

From the Author

I have been listening to god's voice my whole life.
I've found that it comes to me in many ways, some
more mysterious than others, but all of them filled
with love. This book arose out of one of god's voices,
which happened to be that of a small girl, Little
Buddha. I feel so touched that she came to me, and I
hope you enjoy hearing her speak to you through the
words of this book.

Blessings to you,
Rob

Little Buddha Book Five

Little Buddha Book Five

Table of Contents

the person 1

beliefs.. 21

lifeline.. 37

homeschool 57

daydream.. 81

revelations 101

joy 127

new life... 153

leaping 175

arrival 201

questions for going deeper 223

Little Buddha Book Five Notes 245

Little Buddha Book Five

the person

Little Buddha Book Five

the person

I knew there was something wrong the moment I heard the phone ring. I can't explain it, but at some point, an energetic wave hit me.

I reached for the phone receiver and breathlessly said, "Hello."

For a moment there was no sound, then a whisper of a voice and sobbing.

"What's wrong? Who's calling?", I asked, already sensing the answer.

"It's Lynn, Sam." There was a pause, a long deep breath, then she continued, "It's Walt and he's in the ICU in a coma."

There was a lengthy hesitation on my part before responding. I just couldn't find my voice.

"How? Why?", was all I could stammer out.

"It seems he just keeled over. A neighbor was outside and saw Walt go down, like he was falling in slow motion. The neighbor called 911 right away, and it probably saved Walt's life."

"Where is he now?"

2

Little Buddha Book Five

"He's at Memorial Hospital in their ICU, while they're trying to figure out what's wrong with him. Can you come?"

"I'll pack right now and find the fastest way to you. I'll text you my flight information as soon as I have it. Can you pick me up at the airport?"

Lynn said, "Yes", and we ended the call.

Janine and Claire were standing right behind me and asked what had happened.

I explained and we went into action. Janine helped me pack and Claire went on-line to arrange my flight.

After a few minutes Claire came into the bedroom and told me I was all set.

"How'd you do that without my credit card information?", curious to know how a thirteen-year-old could make such quick arrangements.

"Simple, I've got my own credit card, and it went right through," she responded.

Janine nodded to me, as if to say, 'kids these days, huh?'

Little Buddha Book Five

Obviously, she must have co-signed the credit card application, but I was still surprised.

My flight left on time and thankfully there were no problems. I was still uncomfortable, given my past history with flying, but everything was fine. Once off the plane, up the jetway and through the terminal, I finally reached the baggage claim area where Lynn said she'd meet me.

She stood, looking around anxiously for me, then smiled and waved when she spotted me.

We hugged and she brought me up to date.

"Walt is stable, and they think it was a heart attack. You know his father died of the same thing and at about the same age."

I did know that. It had been a long-standing conversation point with him. He'd even joke with me that he was living on borrowed time, make a face and then laugh and say, "Well, what can you do when your number is up."

I never liked it when he talked that way. I liked it even less now.

"Can I see him?" I asked, knowing there are different rules, depending on the hospital.

"I checked and you have to be family, so, no."

I responded, "Walt doesn't have any family, so maybe they'd bend the rules for his best friend."

"You can certainly ask," Lynn said.

About an hour and a half later we pulled up in front of the hospital's main entrance.

"I'll let you out here and go park the car. I'll meet you in the ICU waiting area in a bit."

I said okay and found my way through the hospital until I came upon the ICU Nurses Station.

One of the nurses, Pat, according to her name badge, asked if she could help me. I gave her Walt's name and explained the situation. She looked at me sympathetically, glanced left and right and told me to follow her.

"He's still in a coma but otherwise appears to be in good condition. You can go right in."

Little Buddha Book Five

I opened the door. Walt's eyes were closed, which I expected, but I wasn't prepared for all the machines he was hooked up to.

I pulled up a chair and sat down next to him, careful not to bump into him for fear it might set off some alarm.

I admit that I wished he would open his eyes and talk to me, but he just laid still, quietly breathing.

After an hour or so, I stood up to stretch my legs. I thought I should probably check in with Lynn, but I was afraid I wouldn't get back in to see Walt if there were a change in the nursing staff.

When I turned back around, I thought I saw Walt's eyes twitch. I wasn't one hundred percent sure, but I thought I ought to alert the nurse, so I reached over and hit his call button.

Everything was black. From Walt's point of view, this didn't make any sense. If he was dead, shouldn't he be seeing dazzling white light? And shouldn't figures be approaching him, with wide open arms, ready to hug and welcome him?

Little Buddha Book Five

Wait, Walt noticed there were small rays of light settling around him.

Then he became aware of movement, and it felt as if he were slowly heading forward. In the distance, he saw a bench with a person sitting on it. In the next moment, he was there too. Time was moving very strangely, and it was hard to understand.

The person next to him turned and said, "Hello."

Walt was taken aback. Somehow, he didn't think either of them would be able to speak. Why did he think that?

Walt asked the person, "Where are we?"

The person responded, "Home".

"Home?", Walt repeated.

Walt waited for a moment, looked around and somehow was able to see one scene after another from his life. There wasn't any screen or monitor to see them on, they were just there, and they came in rapid succession and yet he recognized everyone, until one scene appeared that he didn't remember.

Little Buddha Book Five

He asked the person, "What's happening?"

"It's one of your other homes. Give yourself a moment to adjust," the person coached.

Walt thought for a second, closed his eyes, breathed in slowly, then opened his eyes and asked, "Is this from the life before the one I just lived?"

The person responded, "Before, after, it doesn't matter, it never did really."

"What does that mean?", Walt wanted to know.

The person paused considering, then said, "There is really only one life. You're still stuck in lateral time. Don't worry, it will wear off."

Walt repeated questioningly, "Lateral time?"

The person took pity on Walt. "There is no such thing as lateral time, but you used it to differentiate one experience from another. You don't have to do this anymore."

"What do I do now?", Walt asked.

"Release it," the person answered.

Little Buddha Book Five

"Release lateral time?", Walt echoed.

"Yes, perhaps this will help you, it did for me. Imagine that time is vertical, rather than horizontal and that everything happens at the same moment, rather than in a sequence."

"Sorry, that didn't help me at all," Walt stated.

"Okay, let's try this," the person continued, "Imagine lateral time starts at one end of a spectrum and moves forward in a series of event toward the other end of the spectrum."

"I'm okay with that so far," Walt responded.

The person nodded and went on, "Now imagine being able to grasp both ends, and while holding your lateral timeline tightly, you move it from its horizontal axis to its vertical axis. Now instead of events unfolding in a sequence, they're all happening at once."

"What? Really?", Walt stammered.

"I know it's a departure from what you are used to, but it's the truth here," the person said, reassuring Walt with a smile. "If you give yourself a chance, you can open to the way it really is."

9

Little Buddha Book Five

Walt tried to find his voice. "Which is that everything is happening at once?"

The person paused and sighed quietly, "That's the easy version, but it's a good start."

He's doing it again, see, his right eye just twitched," I told the nurse.

"Yes, I saw it too," Pat replied, "Coma patients occasionally have spasms in their bodies. The doctors don't know for sure what it means."

The way she said that seemed suggestive to me, as if she had an opinion she wanted to share, but I'd have to ask her for it.

So, I did, "Pat, I want to know what you think."

She looked at me carefully before responding, "I think they're in another world, one beyond where we are."

"What other world?", I asked, curious to know exactly what she meant.

"I've been a nurse a long time. I've seen humans born and I've seen humans die and there's something very special about each. For

Little Buddha Book Five

a long time, I've sensed they share something in common. I'd call it an 'awareness', I guess. I don't talk about it much because it seems to make others uncomfortable."

She stopped, but I sensed she had more she wanted to say, so I asked, "I'd like to hear more about what you believe," and opened my eyes a little wider, encouraging her to continue.

She glanced into the hallway before saying, "I've been on the ICU for three years now and have seen several coma patients. Most of them have returned and I've listened to their stories. They're anxious to tell me and it seems they are all variations on one theme."

I was extremely curious now, "What theme?"

"Well, what they've told me is that they all feel differently from when they left and that everything has changed for them. Also, every one of them told me it was their decision to come back and that no one else made them do it. Of course, I can't ask those still in comas, but I wonder if maybe they haven't decided what to do yet."

I confess, I'd never thought about this before. I wondered what Walt was experiencing and

Little Buddha Book Five

whether, when he came back, he'd have a story like this to tell.

I corrected myself, 'if' he came back.

"Are there folks still in comas here in this hospital?"

"Just one, She's been in a come the whole time I've been in the ICU. She's a special case, some relative of a hospital board member, so apparently, she can stay here as long as she's alive."

This stunned me. Keeping someone alive, but not knowing if they'd ever regain consciousness. Or, for that matter, what they'd be like if they did.

I wondered what questions they'd ask and who they'd remember. The whole thing was baffling to me.

Walt said, "Well, if that's the easy version, what's the complicated one?" He'd asked, hoping the person could explain more.

"Let's start with this. Presently you're having a 'near life experience'.

Walt interrupted, "Don't you mean a near death experience?"

"No," the person said. "there is no such thing as death. There is only life, but because you are here, you're sort of suspended…you're near life."

"How long do I stay here?" Walt asked, hoping he'd receive an answer that would make sense to him.

The person responded, "That depends."

"On what?"

"On what you decide, of course."

Walt was perplexed, "So, I'm free to choose whether to stay here or go back?"

"Naturally. Do you think it's someone else's decision?"

"Well, yes, I do think that."

The person looked at Walt and smiled, knowing how difficult the conversation was for him. "Walt, it's always your choice. Do you remember the concept of 'free will'?"

Walt thought a moment before responding. "I guess I thought it wasn't real."

The person shook his head knowingly, "Yes, I remember folks like you. You probably accepted what you were taught by others and never questioned things too much."

"That sounds about right," Walt agreed.

"Well, the truth is you really do have a choice. You did then and you do now."

"Free will allows you to experience anything you choose. You were probably taught that only certain options were available to you, right?"

"As I think about it now, my answer is 'yes'. All throughout my life I've believed there would be penalties or punishments if I chose wrong. So, I guess, I just accepted that I was limited, and I tried to fit in as best as I could."

"Did that work for you?", the person wanted to know.

"Honestly, I'm not sure how to answer that question."

"I have an idea," the person said, "are you open to trying something with me?"

"I think so, but I have to admit, I feel quite disoriented at the moment," Walt responded.

"In order to see clearly, you must release what you think you know, because it is only then that you can know the truth."

"That sounds a bit cryptic to me."

"Walt," the person said, while turning to stare directly into his eyes, "let's go for a short trip and I'll show you what I mean."

"Okay," Walt acknowledged, trying to brace himself for this next adventure.

Instantly, they were in a room, surrounded by one single seamless circular wall. A moment later, it came to life and Walt could see a scene shown on it from every direction. Without realizing it, he was in a chair in the middle of the room. Watching the screen like it was a movie.

Walt heard the person's voice, "Without consciously choosing, you've selected this memory to begin your journey."

15

Little Buddha Book Five

The scene was from Walt's childhood. He was looking out the window watching a young girl swinging from a tire suspended from a high branch on a tree next door to his house.

"Do you know where you are?", the person asked.

"Oh, I sure do," Walt answered, strong emotions starting to well up in him.

"What are you thinking?", the person prompted.

"I'm thinking I want to go out and meet her. She's beautiful. But my parents have told me I have to stay away from her and her family. I don't understand why, but every time I see any of them outside, my parents yell at me for even looking at them."

"Keep watching," the person said.

The young girl jumped off the swing and waved to Walt, then said something he couldn't hear.

Walt remembered clearly how important it was. He had to know what she had said, so he looked around and not seeing his parents, slipped out the back door and walked toward her.

Little Buddha Book Five

The young girl smiled at Walt. It was the most beautiful, radiant, magical smile he'd ever seen. He knew it right then, in that moment, she was the one for him.

Walt ran to her, stopping just short of bumping into her and said, "Hi, I'm Walt...you're so pretty!"

He'd felt like a fool for blurting it out like that, but he wasn't embarrassed by what he'd said. Walt watched her carefully for her reaction.

She reached over and kissed him, right on the lips. It was the first real kiss of his life, and he knew two things instantly. One, that he would remember that kiss for the rest of his life and two, that he would find a way to marry her, no matter what his parents said.

The person watched Walt, enjoying the dreamy look on his face, then spoke, "That is free will in action."

Walt stared at the person and nodded. He understood now. Walt smiled and watched as his own story played out in front of him, how he and Cindy were inseparable, wrapped in love, until; she was laid to rest, freed from her suffering and the tyranny of her pain.

Walt thought the movie would end there, but it didn't because as he stood facing her gravestone, she came and wrapped her arms around him and held him close and spoke to him.

"I'm still here with you Walt and I always will be. I know it's hard without me physically by your side, but I don't think your earth life is over yet. The decision is yours, but I believe there's something you still want to do. Am I right, my love?"

Walt felt overwhelmed with emotion. To feel Cindy's presence and feel her as she hugged him from behind, one of her favorite things to do on earth, brought a cascade of tears to him. And he let them come, all of them.

When the flood was over, Walt felt emptied, but instead of feeling filled with sadness, he found joy flowing through him. Cindy was right of course, just as she always had been. He did have something still left to do.

"Look," I shouted, "he just opened his eyes!"

Pat ran into the room and began checking Walt out, She seemed very happy to see the light return to him.

18

"So, back from the dead?" I asked Walt, without thinking.

Walt looked at me, smiled and responded, Nope, back from the life."

I had no idea what he meant, but I didn't care at the moment, I was just glad my best friend had returned.

Little Buddha Book Five

Little Buddha Book Five

beliefs

Little Buddha Book Five

beliefs

A moment after opening his eyes, they closed again, and he promptly fell sound asleep.

Pat put her hand on my shoulder and suggested I go get some rest and come back in the morning. "Things are always better in the morning", she said, as she ushered me out of Walt's room.

I ambled down the hallway and stepped into the ICU waiting room and into Lynn's healing embrace. I shared the wonderful news with her that Walt had awoken, and she screamed with delight and relief. After a few minutes' conversation, I took out my cell to check my messages. The first one I came to was from Janine and Claire telling me I had a reservation at a Marriott three blocks from the hospital. What a pair of angels.

I called Janine and told her the news. Both she and Claire, in the background, cheered and told me how happy they were to hear it. I told them I wanted to stay another day or two so I could spend some time with Walt. They both encouraged me to stay as long as I needed and told me they loved me and to pass along their love to Walt.

Little Buddha Book Five

Lynn drove me to the hotel and asked me to keep her up to speed about my plans, which I promised to do.

I checked in, carried my travel bag up to my room and feel onto the bed and was gone. It felt so reminiscent to me, but I was too tired to remember why.

The next morning, I showered, dressed, had breakfast, and called Lynn to let her know I was going to walk to the hospital, and I'd let her know the rest of my plans later.

When I arrived, I was surprised to see Pat standing at the nurse's station. She discreetly waved me over and told me she'd switched shifts with another nurse so she could have the morning shift, so she could get me in to see Walt.

I was profoundly touched by this generous act and said to Pat, "You're extraordinary and I'm so grateful to you...bless you."

Walt was wide awake and disconnected from everything. He'd proclaimed himself healed and had been telling anyone who would listen that he was ready to leave. After ordering and reviewing a few more tests, the doctors

23

reluctantly agreed, but warned Walt to stay
with someone for the next few days, just to be
on the safe side.

Walt said he had a better idea and asked me
to stay with him. I knew Janine and Claire
would support me, so I agreed, and we called
Lynn for a ride.

She arrived a little later and the three of us
went to Walt's house, after stopping for some
take out from his favorite restaurant.

"So, go ahead," Walt said, "I know you both
have questions. Ask away."

I'd intended to be cautious about approaching
this conversation, but Walt's invitation, paired
with my curiosity, was too much for me.

"What can you tell us about what happened-
anything?", I asked.

Walt said that he couldn't remember it all, then
proceeded to tell us about his conversation
with the person he shared a bench with. Walt
said he wanted to tell us more but was still
processing it himself.

Little Buddha Book Five

"What I can tell you is that I spent time with Cindy and for the first time in years I felt fully alive. It was a dream come true. I swear I felt her hugging me. I never cried so hard."

Lynn was starting to get misty, and I probably was too. I remember how in love they always were and was so happy for him to reexperience that again.

"Seeing her, being with her, it helped me make a decision. It's the reason I've come back."

"Wait, what", Lynn exclaimed, "you mean you had a choice to stay or come back here?"

"Funny," Walt said, "I asked the very same question. Yes, everyone always has that choice. The person I talked with explained it to me. It made sense at the time, but I need to let it sink in more before I can tell you any more about it. Just take it from me, okay?"

"Okay with me," I said, then went on, "so, there was another person there with you?"

"Yeah, and the person was quite enlightening. I can't imagine how disoriented I would have been if I'd been alone."

Little Buddha Book Five

"What's the decision you've come to?", I asked.

"I'm going to put my teaching and administrative skills to work in the field."

"What field?", Lynn and I asked at the same time.

"Among my people." Walt said.

"What people?", Lynn and I chimed in together.

"I've never shared this with anyone before. It seemed too personal, sorry Sam, even to tell you. I am not ashamed of it at all, but I didn't feel worthy enough to say anything."

"The suspense is killing me," I said, "out with it already."

"I am Native American, actually I like the term First People better. My mom was full blooded Montagnese, from Canada and my dad was from Scotland, but had come to live in northern New York. I was born in Chicoutimi, Quebec. No one ever seemed to recognize my heritage. We moved to the US when I was one or two, so I have no memories about living in Canada.

Little Buddha Book Five

And even though I never learned my native language or customs or rituals, my heart has always been with my original tribe."

Walt paused for a moment before continuing, "I'm going home to Canada, hopefully to my kin, but if I can't find them or they don't want me, to another tribe or whoever will have me."

Lynn and I were both stunned, by Walt's revelation and his plans and the suddenness of his decision.

Walt noticed our faces but went on, "I'm going to sell everything but a few things I need and use the proceeds to get there and buy a small place. Whatever is left over I'll use to help in whatever ways I can. My retirement checks will keep me afloat so I can dedicate my time and energy without worrying about finances."

"I don't know if they'll accept me. I feel like an outsider, except for my birthright, but that decision will be up to them."

"If no one wants me, I'll learn what I can and try to help whoever comes to me."

Noble, I thought, just like the man I knew and called my best friend.

27

Little Buddha Book Five

"Is there anything I can do to help?", I asked.

"Not at the moment. I've got a lot of thinking and planning to do. Wait, that's not right," Walt said correcting himself. "I've got a lot of breathing and centering and listening to do."

I'd never heard him talk this way and glanced at Lynn to see if she was picking up the same energy shift I was.

She caught my eye and winked. I guess she had.

Walt noticed her wink and said, "I know, it's like I'm a different person. Well, you know what, I am."

And with that, we all ate heartily, and our conversation took a more lighthearted turn.

For the next several days Lynn and I helped Walt ready his home for sale, pack the things he wanted to take on his trip and talked about all the good times we'd shared together.

During one of our meals, Lynn asked Walt, "I'm curious, what was it like where you were with the person on the bench? Were you afraid?"

28

Little Buddha Book Five

The way Lynn spoke, I got the distinct impression she'd been holding back from asking this question since Walt came out of his coma, like it was critical that she know his answer.

Walt set down his food and seemed to drift off for a moment. "No, I can't say I was ever afraid. Disoriented, for sure, but it was quite peaceful there. I kind of wish I'd been more 'conscious', I guess I'd call it, because there are so many more questions I have. I wish I could still talk more with him. And, you know what's funny, I don't even know the person's name."

"That does seem odd. I guess formal introductions aren't necessary in heaven," I threw in.

As soon as I said it, I wondered if Walt would respond to my use of the word, 'heaven'.

He looked at me and winked, then said, "Not sure if it was heaven, but that doesn't matter to me. It was real in its own way, in a very special way. I'm looking forward to going back and I'm not afraid any more about death. I think others need to know that."

Lynn responded saying, "I'm sure you'd like to spend more time with Cindy when you return."

Walt nodded, smiled, and said, "Yes, I sure would. It's so comforting to know she's there waiting for me."

Changing the subject, I asked, "If you could ask the person one more question, what would it be?"

Walt paused to consider.

He appeared deeply lost in thought, then responded.

"I've spent what seems like my whole life basing my actions on certain beliefs. I know everybody probably does the same thing, but I don't think I ever questioned my beliefs once I decided on them. I never reexamined them or even wondered if there was another way to view life, perhaps a better way."

After a moment, Walt continued, "I feel like I have a second chance at life and I intend to question everything I believe. I want to see where this leads me. I want to understand why I've chosen what I have and see if my decisions truly support me and offer me my best life."

I glanced over at Lynn to check her reaction. She pushed back a little from the dining room table and looked over at me. We shared a look I'd describe as 'surprise', since neither of us had ever heard Walt speak like this before.

"I know," Walt said, "you're both going to have to get used to the new me."

We all laughed, and Walt went on, "There's so much about my life that I don't understand. So many decisions that don't make sense to me and choices I've made that I now see led me deeply into unhappiness."

Lynn picked up this thread and asked, "Do you have an example you're comfortable sharing?"

"The first one that comes to me," Walt said, tilting his head a little in her direction, "is the whole idea of aging. I've always believed that as a person aged, their physical and mental abilities decreased, making it harder for them to maintain good health. It seems to me that folks just deteriorate until they aren't able to do much."

"But now I see that's only true for me if I give my power to this way of thinking. I wonder to myself, why would I want to do that? It occurs to me that, what you believe becomes your truth. And given, I don't want to have my health go downhill just because I get older, I realize I have a choice of believing what best serves me."

Walt's statements made a great deal of sense to me and after thinking a little more about it, I said, "It feels like you could do that with everything. You could question every belief, and if they no longer felt true to you, you could choose a new path, one that aligned with the beliefs that do serve you."

I paused a moment, then went on, "And by serves you, I mean the decisions you make about your beliefs help create your best, most meaningful life."

Walt's eyes lit up and he smiled. "Yes, Sam, and I can help others do the same thing no matter what they've chosen in the past. It's really an extension of what the person told me, that EVERY choice is MINE. I can see and feel how rewarding it could be to assist others in their finding their own new paths through life."

Little Buddha Book Five

Lynn appeared to reflect Walt's smile with one of her own and joined the conversation, "I've been thinking about this whole idea for a while now, wondering if there's a way to be happy with my choices, both when I make them and when I repeat them. I want to be comfortable. I want to see the connections between my choices and their outcomes, and only repeat the decisions and beliefs that lead me to a joyful life. Right now, that's not happening, but it's my biggest desire."

Walt grinned at both of us and offered an idea to consider.

"How about we agree to meet one year from today and share our journey's. We can tell each other how we explored our beliefs, how we made choices to shift them and what outcomes we experienced. How does that sound?"

Lynn and I nodded enthusiastically, and we both answered, "Yes, absolutely!"

I suggested we each pick one belief to target first and share this with each other. They both agreed and we all sat back and finished our meal.

Little Buddha Book Five

A couple of days later Walt said he felt ready for his next step in life and thanked Lynn and me profusely for our help.

"Seriously," Walt said, "I definitely could not have done all of this without you two. You are both Godsends to me."

"It was our pleasure," I said.

Lynn nodded her head in agreement and said, "Okay, I think it's time we shared the belief we most want to focus on, and I'll go first."

She sat forward in her chair and looked at Walt and then at me, "I've always been bothered by the idea, or should I say, the belief, that I am going to run out of time. It plays out in practically everything in my life. I'm always in a rush and it drives me crazy. I'm planning on exploring that and I hope to dig all the way to the bottom. What about you, Walt?"

Walt appeared to be considering his answer, as if he had several beliefs to choose from, but hadn't quite decided.

"I guess the one that comes up the most for me is my belief that there is only so much one person can do. It feels wrong to me. It feels

Little Buddha Book Five

untrue, but every time I get involved in some worthy cause, I get discouraged because it seems hopeless to think one person can solve anything. This is a big deal to me and probably is the belief that's spurring on all of my actions at the moment, even my move to Canada."

I could certainly see that and felt the intensity of his desire to probe this belief.

"What about you, Sam?"

"Well, the belief I want to unveil is the whole idea of deserving. I find I can accomplish a great deal, but what follows in every wake, is the idea that I don't deserve whatever positive outcomes that happen. I've thought about this many times, but never gotten to the bottom of it. To tell you the truth, it really bothers me, so this is an excellent opportunity to shed some light on it and hopefully be able to shift toward a new path."

"Sounds excellent to me," Lynn said.

"I'm in," I responded. And we all hugged to seal the deal.

35

Little Buddha Book Five

lifeline

Little Buddha Book Five

lifeline

It's been three months since I said goodbye to Walt, so when the phone rang, I thought it might be him checking in.

I reached for the receiver, picked it up and heard a voice I was not expecting. It was Lilly, whom I'd seen yesterday at her new bakery.

"Well good morning stranger," I said into the phone.

"Yes, good morning, Sam, did you enjoy the sweet rolls already?"

"As a matter of fact," I responded, "they're all gone. They were so delicious. Are you calling to see if I want some more?"

Lilly laughed before saying, "Well, not exactly. I was hoping you could stop by tomorrow afternoon, sometime after 3pm when business tails off. I have something important I need to talk with you about."

I detected a hint of panic in her voice as I reached for our calendar.

"Sure, that would work for me. It seems that Janine and Claire are setting up at the Community Center all afternoon and won't be home until 5:00pm. Will that give us enough time?"

"Yes, plenty. Oh, thank you, Sam, I'm feeling better already."

We said our goodbyes and I moved on to some chores I'd been trying hard to get to.

I arrived a few minutes early the next day and scouted out the remains in her bakery cases.

Lilly came through the doorway from the kitchen and walked around the end of the counter so she could hug me.

"What's going on Lilly, you sounded a bit frazzled yesterday?"

"Come on out to the back, so we can talk privately."

Lilly led me to her office and shut the door and began bringing me up to date.

Little Buddha Book Five

"My sister, Carol, is having a difficult time with her son, who we all call, Ranger. He just turned fifteen and she says he's fallen in with a pretty tough crowd. He's been in some trouble, nothing too serious yet, but she's afraid it won't stay that way for long.

"I'm sorry to hear that," I said sympathetically.

"Thanks, Sam. Carol's asked me if he could stay with me for a while. Ranger and I have always gotten along very well and have always had fun together. Carol thinks he'd actually come if it was okay with me."

"How do you feel about that," I asked, knowing Lilly didn't have a lot of time to spare, since her business was growing.

"To tell the truth, it would be difficult for me, unless, I have some help."

"I guess that's where I come in?" I asked.

"Well, yes, you and your family. I was hoping that Ranger could become part of Claire's home school group, that Janine could involve him at the Community Center and that you could spend a little time with him. He's always liked writing and I remember you telling me you taught creative writing classes at your high school. I know this is a lot to ask and I'd be happy to talk directly with Claire and Janine, but I wanted to start with you."

Lilly finally wound down, took a deep breath and searched my face for some hint as to what I was thinking, knowing it was a big ask.

"For my part, I'd be happy to help you and Ranger out. I can't speak for Claire and Janine, but I bet they'd be delighted to assist. How about I give them the overview tonight and see what they think?"

"That would be wonderful Sam. Thank you so much," Lilly said, and for your trouble stopping by today, come with me."

We went back through the kitchen, making our way to the front counter, where she reached into the case and brought out three sweet rolls, bagged them, and handed them to me saying, "See that at least two of these make it to you house for your lovely girls."

I told Janine and Claire about Carol's request and they said they were very interested in helping out. I knew Lilly would be pleased, so I called to tell her the news, after we finished our dinner.

"That's fantastic," Lilly said, relief evident in her voice. "I'll call Carol and tell her the good news. Once I know the plan, I'll get back to you. Again, Sam, thank you so much…and thank Janine and Claire for me please."

A few days later, Carol, and a reluctant Ranger arrived. Lilly opened the front door, came out onto her porch, and waved as they got out of the car. Carol ran to her sister and hugged her, hard.

Whispering, she said, "I'm so sorry, he's barely spoken to me the whole trip. He's really angry with me and I'm afraid he's going to take it out on you once I leave.

Carol let go and called out in a commanding voice to Ranger, "Please come say hi to your aunt."

Lilly wished she hadn't done that and just allowed Ranger to choose his own greeting.

Ranger reached into the car, pulled out his backpack and ambled slowly toward Lilly.

Little Buddha Book Five

"Hello, Ranger, it's so good to see you again, I've missed you."

Ranger hugged Lilly briefly and managed to say, "I've missed you too, but I have to tell you this whole thing sucks," leaving no doubt about how he felt.

Carol stayed through dinner and then left for home. She tried to have one more talk with Ranger, but he waved goodbye and stomped upstairs to his room.

Carol and Lilly exchanged looks, then Carol began sobbing. Lilly hugged her and told her everything would end up to be okay. She didn't have any idea how, but she knew it would.

In truth, she did know, because Lia had assured her it would and Lilly completely trusted Lia now. Maybe one day she'd be able to introduce her to Carol.

Once Carol's crying ended, Lilly walked her to her car, and they said their farewells and promised to keep in touch.

After cleaning up from dinner Lilly went upstairs and knocked on Ranger's door. She felt it would be best not to say anything about his not saying goodbye to her sister, but she needed to tell Ranger about their schedule for tomorrow.

"Can I come in?", Lilly asked.

"It's your house, so I suppose so," was Ranger's reply.

Lilly opened the door and sat in a chair opposite Ranger, who was laying on the bed.

"I imagine this is hard for you, being displaced, away from your friends and familiar surroundings. Maybe, if you give this a chance, you might end up liking it here. I do have to tell you; I need your help at the bakery. Business is so good I need another baker and I remember how much fun we had when you were little making sweet treats. It's part of the reason I'm still doing it."

Lilly paused for a reaction, but Ranger kept laying there, waiting for what was coming.

Lilly continued, "Tomorrow, bright and early, we'll go together to the bakery, and I'll show you around, then we can start making some goodies."

Little Buddha Book Five

Ranger gave Lilly a questioning look and asked, "How early?"

"In order to have fresh baked goods for opening, we have to leave at 4:00am."

Lilly tried to prepare herself for his explosion.

Ranger said nothing at first, then glared up at her, "You've gotta be kidding me. I'm a prisoner here, away from all of my friends and now I'm going to be slave labor starting in the middle of the night." He turned over and ended by saying, "Not a chance."

Lilly stood but made no move to leave his room. She was dazed and saddened by his reaction, even while expecting it. He'd never spoken to her this way.

She paused to consider things from his perspective. What he said was true and not only that, but he was also probably still missing his father, who'd died about a year ago.

What could she do to help him?

"Ranger, I'm sorry things have worked out this way for you. I don't know how you feel you, but

Little Buddha Book Five

I'm going to be here to listen, whenever you want to talk."

Lilly waited a moment to see if he wanted to respond. He didn't.

"I'm sure it is true what you say, but I'm still hoping you'll give me a chance. I'll wake you up at 4:00am and you can let me know. Good night, Ranger, see you in the morning."

Lilly walked out of his room, knowing it was unlikely he'd respond.

When her alarm clock began beeping, she rolled over, got out of bed, and started her morning routine. Once complete, she padded down the hallway and knocked on Ranger's door. No answer. She called out gently, but still no answer.

Lilly knocked a little harder, but without effect. She wondered how he would react if she opened the door. Badly, she imagined, but she felt she had to do it.

Lilly turned the knob and quietly opened the door. As it swung open the first thing she saw was the empty bed. She started to panic and

Little Buddha Book Five

pushed the door all the way, until it banged against the wall. There was no evidence he'd even been there. The room looked completely undisturbed. He was gone and so were his things. What was she going to do now? Nearing hysteria, she picked up the phone and called Sam.

He answered on the third ring, and with grogginess in his voice, said hello.

"Sam, it's Lilly I'm so sorry to call you, but I need your help- please." She stretched out the word 'please', pleading frantically.

Now fully awake Sam said, "Of course, what's wrong?"

Lilly explained and Sam reassured her, saying he'd get right into action.

"Can you text me his photo, so I'll know it's him, if I can find him?"

Lilly agreed and a moment later, Sam's phone dinged.

"Got it," Sam stated, "I'll start searching as soon as I'm dressed, and I'll keep you posted."

47

Little Buddha Book Five

Janine was awake now and asked Sam what was going on. He explained and they decided she'd go to stay with Lilly once Claire was up and while Sam tried to find him.

After a few minutes Sam went downstairs to get a cup of coffee, his keys, and a jacket.

Sitting, waiting for him was his beautiful daughter, Claire.

Surprised, Sam asked, "What are you doing up honey?"

"I'm going with you to help you find Ranger, I thought you could use an extra set of eyes."

Janine came down the stairs, saw Claire fully dressed and immediately understood the situation.

"You two better get going, I'm sure Lilly is pretty upset. I'll take my car and keep her company and reassure her all will be well."

I guessed that meant she'd given her blessing, so Claire and I headed to my car, got in, and started discussing where Ranger might have gone.

48

Little Buddha Book Five

"It's 4:15 am, where could he be?", I said aloud.

"I've been thinking about that," Claire responded, "and I have a few ideas. I'd want to be warm, dry, relatively safe and it would have to be a place that is open this early. If it was me, I'd go to a laundromat."

"Brilliant, that's the perfect place. I know about two, do you know if there are more around here?"

Claire sat forward in her seat, turned toward me, and stated, "The closest one to Lilly's house is the one on Main Street, several blocks from down from her bakery. They would have seen it on their way into town, so maybe he'd remember it."

As usual, her awareness of the obvious was right on point. "Let's try there first," I said, while making a turn in that direction.

"Do you know what he looks like?", Claire asked.

I handed her my phone, "Yes, I had Lilly text me his picture."

Little Buddha Book Five

"Good thinking Dad."

It only took us two minutes to reach the 'All Day Any Day' laundromat. I parked right out front, we both got out and headed toward the front door.

Claire placed a hand gently on my forearm and stopped walking. I did the same, knowing she wanted to tell me something.

"Please don't take this the wrong way, but I think you need to let me be the one to go in alone."

Instantly, I felt a protective surge, after all I'd never met Ranger and couldn't possibly know how he'd react to strangers coming up to him. But I could see something in Claire's eyes. A certainty, a knowingness. I'd seen it a hundred times before, so I acquiesced.

"Okay, but I'll be right here if you need me."

She reached for my hand, squeezed it and told me not to worry.

Claire opened the door and stood just inside scanning the large room filled with washers, dryers, and areas to fold clothes. She looked toward the back of the room where a row of chairs was lined up close to the rear exit. There, in the last chair was Ranger sitting with his eyes closed and his ear buds snugly secured in his ears.

Claire slowly approached and sat next to him but didn't say or do anything.

Despite this, Ranger's eyes opened and with a startled expression he turned toward Claire and asked, "What are you doing here?"

Claire motioned to Ranger to take his ear buds out, then responded, "I came to talk to you."

Completely taken aback, Ranger eyed her closely. Beautiful girl, he thought, but why is she really here? And why would she be here to talk with him? What kind of crazy person stops by a laundromat at this time of day? None of this made any sense to him.

"What do you want to talk about," Ranger stammered.

"I thought we could talk about the whole idea of homeschooling."

Little Buddha Book Five

"Are you demented or something? It's 4:30 in the morning and you want to talk about homeschooling with me in this empty laundromat?"

"Where are your clothes?", Claire asked.

"What?"

"Well, as you've pointed out, this is a laundromat. It's where people wash and dry their clothes, so where are yours? It's a pretty simple question don't you think?"

Ranger couldn't deny her logic and couldn't think of a good response, so said nothing and just stared at her.

"Do you want to know what I think?" Claire asked.

Who was this insane person, Ranger wondered. "Whatever", was his eventual response.

"Wonderful. I think all of your clothes are already clean, but you wanted a safe dry, warm place to hang out while you planned your next move."

Little Buddha Book Five

Claire eyed him and asked, "So far, so good?"

Annoyed at her presuming to know anything about him, he answered, "Not exactly," grumpiness evident in his voice.

"Really," Claire responded, "then maybe you can fill me in."

"Why should I?" Ranger said testily, "I don't owe you anything."

Claire, refusing to take his bait offered, "That's where you're wrong."

"What do you mean by that?", he said quickly, wondering why he was so angry with her. She was nothing to him. But somehow, he wanted to know more about her and to discover the real reason she was here with him.

"We're all each other's lifeline," Claire responded, while smiling at him.

"What makes you think I need a lifeline?"

"Because you are human. You are human, aren't you?"

"Duh, yes, I'm human," Ranger answered.

Claire went on, "Every human needs something. Actually, we need a lot of things. We can't always have what we want, but if we grab onto lifelines offered to us by others, our chances really improve. You can do that for me, and I can do that for you. Someday I may need what you have to offer and someday you may need what I have to offer."

Claire stopped to gauge his reaction, watching him carefully. There was a spark in his eye that hadn't been there when they'd begun their conversation.

"And I suppose you're going to tell me, you are my lifeline today?", Ranger said, wondering if she truly meant what she was saying.

"Wow, look who is paying attention. Yes, that's exactly what I'm telling you. I'm here to offer you a way forward."

"Is that where homeschooling comes in?", he asked without his usual irritated tone.

"Another point for you, my new friend. Yes, that's where homeschooling comes in. But first, I'd like to make you a deal."

Little Buddha Book Five

Somewhat warily Ranger asked, "What kind of deal?"

"The kind where we work a little, then play a little."

"I don't understand, what do you mean?"

"Well, I thought maybe you and I could learn how to be bakers this morning, then I'll show you around town and introduce you to my homeschool buddies. I'm pretty sure you'd like them, and I know they'd like you. We're planning an event for next week and we could use your unique set of skills. I know you have lots of questions. How about this? How about we go to your aunt's bakery first and while we learn to make tasty treats, you can ask me anything you want?"

"So, you know my aunt already, don't you?"

"Sure, everyone in town does, her baked goods are pretty famous. I've always wanted to know how she makes them, and this is a great chance to learn. What do you say?"

Ranger mulled this over. He did have a lot of questions for this girl, and she was great to look at. And maybe her friends might be fun, although he admitted, he hoped they were more normal than her. His curiosity won out.

"I don't pretend to understand what's happening here, but I guess I'm in."

Claire stood, offered Ranger her hand, and said, "Here's a lifeline for you."

Surprisingly, Ranger reached out and took her hand in his and stood.

homeschool

Little Buddha Book Five

homeschool

It turns out that they had a wonderful time with Lilly, baking, talking and of course, sampling the fruits of their labor.

Lilly could see how good Claire was for Ranger and how she brought out his happy-go-lucky personality, which she thought he might have lost.

When Sam came to pick Claire up, he asked whether Lilly and Ranger would be available to come to dinner.

Lilly glanced at Ranger to see his reaction and discovered an unexpected smile creasing his face. He nodded 'yes' to her and she accepted.

"I'll bring a treat for dessert, if that's okay with you."

Claire and Sam immediately agreed to her offer, and everyone exchanged goodbyes.

At 5:30, Lilly and Ranger joined Janine, Claire, Sam, and Claire's homeschool buddy, Jamie and her father, Dave, for dinner.

Little Buddha Book Five

After introductions, everyone picked up a plate and circled around the serving table, which was set up as a buffet.

Ranger thought to himself that it had been a long time since he had this many food items to choose from. His mom was a good cook, but she had to work long hours and by the time she got home, was pretty tired, certainly too tired to make anything like this.

Once everyone filled their plates, they sat down at the large dining room table. Ranger was surprised to be seated between Claire and Jamie. It was difficult for him not to stare at each of them. He couldn't decide who was more beautiful. Did they grow them on trees here or something. None of his friends even came close to their kind of gorgeous. He actually felt a bit self-conscious, like everyone was staring at him, knowing what he was thinking, and it unnerved him.

"Did you enjoy baking?", Janine asked Ranger and Claire.

"I loved it, "Claire responded, "especially the sampling part."

Little Buddha Book Five

When Ranger didn't answer right away. Claire gently nudged him in the ribs.

"Oh, yeah, it was fine," he offered.

"They were both really helpful," Lilly put in, "and it would be great to have them help whenever they could."

Clearly, she was relieved by her nephew's mood change and his openness to accepting the dinner invitation. She was also grateful for the opportunity for him to get to know other people, especially those his own age.

"Ranger, do you think you could take a day off from baking to help Claire and me out tomorrow?"

This question came from Jamie and was the first time she'd spoken.

Ranger thought to himself, she had an enchanting voice to go along with the rest of her.

He noticed she didn't turn toward him to ask her question, which seemed odd. He looked more carefully at her and how she moved with a kind of precision he'd never seen before.

60

Little Buddha Book Five

And before he knew it, he blurted out, "Are you blind or something?"

He immediately regretted saying this and tried to cover up his awkwardness with a laugh.

But instead of taking offense, she simply answered, "Yes, to both."

Her response confused him. Both?

As if able to anticipate his reaction, she continued, "Yes, I am blind, and yes, I am something."

She emphasized the words, 'I am'.

Ranger felt even more confused but couldn't think of a way to ask a follow up question.

Claire came to his rescue, offering another lifeline.

"Jamie may be physically blind, but she sees more than anyone I've ever met. If I have trouble figuring things out, I'll often ask her, and she always has something of value to say."

Little Buddha Book Five

Jamie reached out her hand for a high-five and Claire slapped it. "Thanks, my friend, back at you."

With the tension gone, Ranger relaxed. He realized why he hadn't noticed right away. She didn't walk with a cane, didn't wear dark glasses, or put her hands out in front of her to feel where she was going, like other blind people he'd seen. He also noticed she ate the same way he did and seemed 'perfectly normal'. How could she do all that? As he considered this, he became even more impressed with her. It was then he noticed he was staring at her and quickly looked away. He wondered if anyone had seen.

Everyone had, but no one said anything.

"So?", asked Jamie again.

He'd forgotten what she'd asked him. It was like he was stuck in a dream. Claire seemed unusual, kind of cool, but Jamie was indeed 'something'.

Without knowing what he was agreeing to, he just said, "Yeah, sure."

Little Buddha Book Five

Jamie nodded and suggested they get together at her house around nine the next morning, then tilted her head in Dave's direction for confirmation that it would be okay.

Dave said, "Yes", and Claire and Ranger both agreed.

The rest of the meal was both delicious and entertaining.

Ranger was particularly interested in the things Jamie's father, Dave, had to say. He'd always been interested in science and technology, so could follow most of what Dave was telling everyone, that is until he started explaining his newest discovery.

Sam had asked Dave whether he had any revelations during his 'night school' sessions. Dave explained, his voice becoming more animated with each passing minute he spoke.

Dave turned his attention toward Ranger and continued, "My night school is when I create in my mind a subject or idea, I want more clarity about and I fix it deeply by repeating it over and over until I fall asleep. My concept is that this repetition forms a link between my waking conscious mind and my sleeping subconscious

Little Buddha Book Five

mind. It's like setting up a bridge between them so information can flow."

Ranger interrupted, "Wait, are you saying you can program your dreams?"

"Yes, that would be fair to say," Dave answered. "You see, once I've introduced a singly focused question or concept, I find the door swings wide open during the night and I receive insights that inform my daytime actions and research."

Ranger surprised himself by responding, "That's fascinating." He'd completely forgotten about being angry about his displacement from his home or his separation from his friends. Maybe he was going to like it here, just as his aunt had said.

"So, what was your subject…the question you wanted answered?", Ranger asked, clearly focused now directly on Dave.

"That's going to take a few minutes to explain, and I don't want to hog the conversation." Dave glanced around the table and his surprise was evident. Everyone was looking at him and smiling.

Little Buddha Book Five

Ranger was the first to speak, "Please, go on, I really want to hear what you have to say."

Lilly appeared very surprised by his sudden intensity but was pleased he seemed more like his former self and joined in by saying, "Yes, please Dave, go ahead, I'm curious too."

Dave shrugged, laughed, mostly to himself, and began again.

"I had the essence of a potentially profound insight about the web of creation, so I concentrated all my energy on this concept before falling asleep the other night and this is what showed up the next morning."

Dave's enthusiasm was mounting, and his characteristically slow deliberate speech had given way to a quicker, more effusive style.

"It's very difficult to explain my understanding of the web of creation because it's so visually stunning. It defies the use of words, so I'll try to describe the image I see as best as I can. You have to understand how frustrating this is to me as a scientist. To see something so meaningful but have no directly tangible way to convey the information."

Little Buddha Book Five

"Enough with the preamble Dad," Jamie stated, "get on with the show."

Everyone laughed, especially Dave.

"Of course, you're right, thanks for the gentle nudge."

Everyone laughed again, which seemed to set the stage properly for Dave's description.

"I know it's going to be different for each of us but try to close your eyes and visualize one layer of points of light stretching out in front of you and spreading out beyond the horizon."

Dave waited a minute or so before continuing. "Each one of the points of light is a choice and each choice point of light is connected, not only to the point closest to it, but to every other point of light."

Before he continued further, Dave looked at each person's face to see their expression. Judging from their rapt attention he sensed they were all engaged.

"Now imagine there is another layer of points of light above and below the first one...do you see it?"

Little Buddha Book Five

Heads nodded, but no one spoke.

"Okay, here's where it gets kind of bizarre. As best you can, imagine expanding the number of layers in all directions."

Dave waited and watched for signs of recognition on their faces. As he scanned, moving from one to another, he had an inner sense that each of them was connecting with the same image he had.

"Hold this image and imagine the web expanding and contracting as you breathe. Allow yourself to be a part of this by choosing one point of light to represent you. As you inhale, the points become closer to you and as you exhale, they move away from you.

Again, Dave provided time for the others to experience their own version of his dream. After giving them ten minutes more he said, "Now begin to come back to this house, this room, this body, this moment...and gently open your eyes."

Dave watched each person's facial expressions very carefully and catalogued them in his mind to process later. He'd often had a mirror present to look at his own

Little Buddha Book Five

expressions once he came out of one of his sessions. He'd become familiar with how he looked and realized it was always much the same and very different from any other times he looked in the mirror or saw his reflection elsewhere.

He noted how peaceful they all looked. Serene would be his best word of description.

Lilly was the first to speak, "Dave, that was amazing! I felt like I was witnessing creation itself. Every time I breathed in and out it felt like the universe expanded and I got bigger."

Her use of the word, 'I' seemed absolutely correct to him and echoed his own experience.

"Me too," Janine added, while the others nodded their confirmations.

"It was surreal," Ranger managed to say, clearly still sensing the effects of Dave's demonstration. "Is it always like that?"

Dave responded, "I don't believe anyone of us experienced the exact same thing, that would defy my sense that we each create the web in our own way. But I suspect we all share some

68

key points, which makes conversing about it rather enjoyable."

A vibrant and enthusiastic conversation ensued, with everyone contributing their own observations and experiences.

At the end of the night everyone agreed it had been a thoroughly pleasurable time.

As the group parted, Dave said, "Sweet dreams everyone," which drew a long ripple of laughter.

Claire knocked on Lilly's front door and waited for Ranger to answer. She couldn't hear any sounds, so she knocked again.

"Coming", she heard Ranger announce, accompanied by heavy footsteps approaching the door. He opened it and told Claire he'd be with her in a minute.

Claire hummed as she waited, raising, and lowering her voice and having fun.

Ranger came back into view and said, "Ok, ready to go."

Little Buddha Book Five

Claire turned and started down the front walkway and headed to the right upon reaching the sidewalk.

Ranger asked, "What were you humming?"

"Nothing in particular. I just like the way the sound feels to me."

This girl was definitely different from any other girl he'd ever known, not that he'd known that many.

"Where are we going?", he asked, curious about their destination.

"Actually, not too far. We're headed to Jamie's house and there will probably be eight or nine of us this morning."

"I guess it would be helpful if you could give me a clue about what happens in a homeschool."

"What would you like to know?", Claire asked.

"Well, for one, who is the teacher?"

Claire smiled and answered, "We don't have one."

Little Buddha Book Five

"What? How can you have a school with no teacher?", Ranger asked, baffled by the concept, but also intrigued.

"The way ours works is that we meet with a counselor, sort of like a teacher, but we only see them four or five times a year, rather than every day, like you would at your school."

This idea sounded good to Ranger, who'd recently had issues with all of his teachers.

"Then who grades you?", he asked, trying to better understand.

"No one does," Claire responded, knowing full well how foreign a concept this would be to him. She enjoyed watching his reactions.

No way," Ranger said, once again finding the idea surprising and appealing at the same time.

"Yes way," Claire stated, "if there were to be any grades, we'd do that ourselves. But the whole idea is to 'learn' about new things and how they connect with what we already know, so that we extend our understanding."

"How do you learn new things?"

71

Little Buddha Book Five

"All kinds of ways. It sort of depends on the subject matter or the projects we decide to pursue."

"Okay, so what are you working on today?"

"We haven't decided yet. That's why we're meeting. You could call it a planning session, I guess."

Despite his previous reluctance, Ranger was very interested in this kind of school, especially the part about no teachers."

It only took about fifteen minutes to arrive at Jamie's house and after ringing her doorbell and going inside, they settled into two comfortable chairs in the living room.

Since it was her house, Jamie was the leader today.

"Let's start with some introductions, starting with you, Claire."

As they went around the circle everyone said their name and something about themselves. Next to Claire was Ranger, then Natalie, Mary, Patricia, Amy, Elijah, Ty, Chase, then Jamie.

Little Buddha Book Five

Ranger would have liked a heads-up regarding having to say something about himself, but it turned out okay.

A wide-ranging discussion took place and almost everyone had a great idea to contribute.

Ranger asked the group, "Does everybody always do the same project, or can we split up?"

Jamie responded first, "We really don't have any rules about that. You can join anyone else or do your own thing. What's important here is to learn something new and be able to share it in a way others can understand and benefit from. Did you have an idea about what you wanted to do?"

Ranger watched Jamie as she spoke, mesmerized by her. If it was possible, she seemed more beautiful this morning than she did last night.

"I do. I'd like to work with your father, researching his 'night school' dreaming thing. Do you think he'd want to help me?"

Little Buddha Book Five

The others in the group, except for Claire and Natalie, seemed unaware of Jaime's father's project, but waited for her to respond before asking for details.

"We could ask him and see what he says. He has a lot going on right now, but he might say 'yes' anyway."

Jamie recognized the group as a whole didn't know about her father's project, so she brought them up to speed. They all seemed very interested and thought it would make a great group venture.

"Maybe your dad would teach all of us and we could help him with his research," Elijah said, while the rest of the group nodded enthusiastically.

"Well, I guess that does it, I'll ask him tonight at dinner and let you know. Is anyone interested in some coffeecake?"

There were more affirmative head nods as everyone got up and headed toward the kitchen.

Jamie led the way, but Chase pushed past her, almost knocking her down.

Little Buddha Book Five

"Yo, jerk, what's up with shoving Jaime out of the way?", Ranger said, shouting at him.

Chase turned abruptly and started to come toward Ranger aggressively.

Without hesitation Ranger made a fist and began to swing his arm forward to punch Chase in the face.

Before his fist managed to connect, Jamie reached out, and with lightning speed, caught his hand in mid motion, and held it there.

Shocked, Chase stood motionless, unable to comprehend both Ranger's attempted punch and Jamie's deft block.

For his part, Ranger was stunned by how swiftly Jamie had reached out and caught his arm. He wondered how that was even possible. How could this blind girl know his intention, sense his action, and locate his arm in thin air? He couldn't make any sense of it.

He stared at Jamie, then at Chase and then at Claire, who stood behind him.

Little Buddha Book Five

Claire noticed the puzzlement on Ranger's face and despite the gravity of the situation, cracked a smile.

"No, no violence in my home," Jamie said emphatically, breaking the silence and some of the tension.

"How?", was all Ranger could stammer.

Chase seemed to come out of the fog he'd been in and repeated Ranger's question, "Yeah, how?"

Jamie stood quietly, breathing in and out slowly, over, and over until she could hear Chase and Ranger settling into their own peaceful breathing patterns.

"If you must know, I could sense the hostility between you two from the moment you both arrived, so I was mentally prepared for this. Then, when you, Chase, pushed past me, I anticipated Ranger's reaction and could feel the tension and hear your movements and knew what you were about to do. Ranger, you are left-handed, about my height, and knowing your position and proximity to me, I simply reached out and caught your hand where I expected it to be, and before your punch could reach Chase."

Ranger thought to himself, okay maybe that was all possible somehow, but he had to ask, "But how were you able to move so fast? I didn't even see your hand move until I felt it." Somehow, he needed to understand this.

As it happens so did Chase, because he asked much the same thing a moment later.

In response, Jamie said, "Training mostly. But also, some intuition and a strong desire to prevent violence."

"Also, what you both ought to know is that there was no need for violence. It never solves anything and only serves to perpetuate itself. Violence begins with two or more people taking things personally. Ranger, you acted the part played by all folks who feel it necessary to react to every perceived 'wrong' someone does to them or someone they care about. Chase, you pushed past me because you wanted to be first in the kitchen, to get the 'best' refreshments. Your aggression in this case means you believe there isn't enough for everyone, so you wanted to get yours first.

77

Little Buddha Book Five

This is the beginning of every war and every act of violence."

Jamie continued, "I have a suggestion for both of you, do you want to hear it?"

Chase and Ranger exchanged looks, nodded to each other, and responded, "Yes."

"If my dad agrees to our night school idea and says he has time to work with us, maybe each of you could explore why you both feel the need for aggression."

"I already know," Ranger said, "because everyone is always telling me what to do. I take after my dad. They call him a brawler, because he would fight anyone at any time, even if they were bigger than him."

"It's sort of the same thing for me," Chase said, "except it's more about getting all the good stuff first, then holding on to it. In my family, if you don't grab something first, you may not get anything at all."

Jamie titled her head toward Ranger and Chase and said, "Let's finish this in the kitchen."

Little Buddha Book Five

Chase was closest but chose to step out of the way and let Jamie go first, then stayed back and let Ranger follow her.

Ranger had been feeling upset with himself, because he knew he was just acting out the way he'd seen his father behave. "I'm sorry Jamie. I wish I wasn't this way; I just can't seem to change."

Chase apologized too, "Yeah, I'm sorry too. I've been here enough times to know you always have plenty of refreshments. I don't know what got into me to push you. I just thought I had enough room. But it was wrong of me no matter what."

"I accept both of your apologies and my suggestion about night school is not meant as any kind of punishment. I honestly believe that if you held the focus I spoke about, certain things would become clear to you."

"I'm game, if your dad is okay about helping us," Ranger said.

"Me too," Chase added.

"Okay, it's settled. How about you two shake hands...and mean it."

79

Little Buddha Book Five

Ranger and Chase conceded, extended their hands, and shook.

Hearing the conversation conclude, Claire and the others joined them in the kitchen. Moments later there was the sound of laughter, Chase and Ranger included.

daydream

Little Buddha Book Five

daydream

"Dad says you can come over tomorrow, if you have the time and still want to," Jamie said over the phone to Ranger.

"That's awesome, I'd love to, What time?"

"How does 10:00am sound?"

"Perfect. I'm sure my aunt won't mind. I'll ask her when she gets home, but I don't think it will be a problem."

Jamie said, "Great, but if she does, please let me know, otherwise, I'll see you then."

"Wait Jamie, are you okay with my apology really?". Ranger felt he had to know for sure.

"I am," she responded, "I sense your honesty and appreciate it."

"Thanks, that's great because I want you to like me."

As soon as he said the words, he wished he could take them back. They sounded so lame to him. What must she think of him?

Little Buddha Book Five

"I do like you Ranger," she said, with some warmth in her voice.

Ranger felt himself melting. She'd just said she liked him. He hadn't expected that since he'd made such a jerk of himself yesterday. It took a minute to realize she was speaking again.

"Give yourself a break about yesterday, okay? It was one single moment in time and it's over unless you decide to carry it with you. Imagine if each time you made a mistake, you had to carry it around with you. Can you imagine how much you would weigh after a while?"

"In my case it would be tons," Ranger responded, meaning it literally.

"You see, letting go keeps you light and airy and open for anything."

"That sounds fantastic," Ranger said, evidently appreciating Jamie's views on life. "Thanks for talking with me."

Jamie concluded their conversation by saying, "You are most welcome. I'll see you tomorrow at 10:00am."

Little Buddha Book Five

They hung up and Ranger sat in his chair
replaying her words, "I do like you, Ranger."
Wow, how things had changed in just the last
two days.

The next morning came quickly, and Ranger
was up and ready to go by 8:00am. Now he
had almost two hours to wait. What was he
going to do? A thought came to him, so he got
out his cell phone and searched for local
flower shops. There was one right on Main
Street and it opened at 9:00am, plenty of time
to pick something out and get to Jaime's
house by 10:00am.

He didn't have much money, but Lilly had
loaned him some, since he was planning on
working for her starting tomorrow. It seemed
she wanted him to spend time with his new
friends and was doing everything possible to
encourage him. She really was a terrific aunt.

Another thought occurred to him as he left the
house and locked the door.

"What kind of flowers did you have in mind?',
the lady behind the counter asked.

Little Buddha Book Five

"I don't have any idea, "Ranger answered blankly. He wished he knew more than he did. Actually, he often wished this.

Taking pity on him, the clerk helpfully asked several questions and formed a few ideas, offering to show Ranger his options.

"That one," Ranger exclaimed, when the clerk brought out the first arrangement. "That's beautiful and I think she'd like it. But I need two of those."

Amused, the clerk smiled, told Ranger the price and turned to get the second arrangement.

"Wait," Ranger said, "I don't have that much money with me. Could I pay you the rest soon?"

He knew it was a long shot. Why would she give credit to some fifteen-year-old kid she didn't know?

"Are you working?", she asked.

"I start tomorrow. I'm working at my aunt Lilly's bakery.

"The new one down the block?", she asked, sounding more interested now.

"Yes. We make some really great stuff."

"Oh, I know, everything I've brought home from there is delicious. You're really Lilly's nephew?"

"I sure am. I promise I'll pay you as soon as I get my first paycheck. Is it a deal?"

The clerk grinned but seemed to be thinking about something.

Ranger broke in, "It would really help me out. One of the arrangements is for her."

"Really," the clerk exclaimed, "how sweet. And the other one?"

"It's for a girl I just met."

"You're buying flowers for a girl you just met?", the clerk asked, surprised by his generosity.

"Yeah, she's really something and I was a total jerk yesterday, so it's sort of an apology."

Little Buddha Book Five

"Okay, you've sold me. I'll box them up right now and you can owe me the difference."

Ranger was thrilled, then taking a chance, asked if the one for his aunt could be delivered later, maybe around 3:00pm when her bakery traffic slowed down, so she could enjoy them.

"What a thoughtful guy you are. I think the girl you're buying these for is pretty lucky."

Ranger flushed red, clearly having never had anyone other than his mother and aunt say anything this nice to him.

"Thanks," was all he could manage to say.

As Ranger stood at Jamie's front door, he suddenly realized what he had done. He'd bought beautiful flowers for a blind girl. How was she supposed to enjoy them when she couldn't see them. Yet one more bad decision in his life, he thought.

Well, I'm here, there's no turning back now he concluded.

He reached up and rang the doorbell.

A moment later it opened and there she stood looking more gorgeous than the last time he'd seen her. How did she do that?

"Oh, Ranger, you didn't need to bring me flowers", she said smiling, but of course I love them. They smell wonderful and I have just the right spot for them. Come in."

Shocked, Ranger walked in and watched as Jamie navigated perfectly to an open spot on a side table, placing the arrangement there. She turned and came toward him, then wrapped her arms around him, hugged him and said, "Thank you so much."

This must be what heaven feels like he thought to himself. Having Jamie hug him was the very best thing that had ever happened to him, not that there had been that many. He wished it would last forever.

"Um, I'm glad you like them," Ranger managed to say, almost whispering.

Jamie released Ranger and said, "My dad will be up in a minute, he's finishing up an experiment in the basement. Why don't we sit on the couch while we wait."

Little Buddha Book Five

A moment later the door to the basement opened and Dave appeared.

"So nice to see you again Ranger," he said, while walking forward with his hand outstretched.

Ranger stood, took Dave's offered hand, and shook it.

"Good strong grip," Dave said, "that tells me everything I need to know."

This man really was so different from anyone he'd ever met Ranger thought. What could a handshake tell anyone?

As if to answer his unasked question, Dave started speaking, "Everyone shakes hands in their own way. Some use only their hand, while others engage their whole body, their eyes, their posture, their energy. You brought your whole self to it, which tells me that when you decide something, you're all in. Now I know you're the right person to help me with a project I have in mind, that is if you want to."

All this from one handshake. How was that possible, Ranger wondered?

"Well, that and the flowers you brought for Jamie."

Had Dave noticed the flowers already? Wow, this man was very perceptive. Maybe that's where Jamie got it from.

"Yes, I'd love to be a part of any project you're doing sir."

Dave looked at Ranger and laughed.

"There are no sirs here, just me. Please call me Dave, or if you prefer, the mad professor," Dave said winking at Ranger.

"My dad is a big kidder. You'll get used to him someday," Jamie said.

"I sure hope so," Ranger replied, then added, "what is the project about?"

"Oh, I think you'll find it very interesting. Come with me both of you and I'll explain."

Dave led them down the stairs to his basement 'lab', which consisted of three large stuffed chairs big enough for two people each set at two, six and ten o'clock positions, so that no chair faced another, but conversation would still be easy.

Have a seat you two, separately of course. Jamie laughed, having heard her father's humor her whole life.

Once they were all seated, Dave began.

"This is a preliminary experiment, but one that will set the stage perfectly."

Dave paused and looked at Ranger, then Jamie, his face difficult to read. It was as if he was calculating something.

"Please close your eyes. Now breathe in and out a few times, each time slowing a bit."

Dave waited until Jaime and Ranger appeared relaxed.

"Okay, what I'd like you to do is bring to mind a recent event where you lost control. It could be physical, emotional, or intellectual control. I'll give you a minute to capture the image. When you have it, bow your head slightly forward, so I'll know you're ready."

Little Buddha Book Five

Ranger had no trouble choosing a recent event where he'd lost control. It was in the house upstairs, yesterday. The image quickly formed in his mind, and he bowed his head. He wondered how long it would take Jamie to come up with something, as calm and collected as she was. Had he known that she had her head already bowed, he'd have been surprised.

After what seemed like a few minutes, Dave began speaking again.

"While continuing to breathe slowly and peacefully, choose one word to describe your event...only one word. Now, go beneath this word until you find a deeper word, one that exists below your first word."

Ranger was confused. A deeper word, what did that mean? But just as he thought that a word did come to him. This surprised him. He'd never seen any connection until now.

"What would allow these words to disappear?" Dave asked. "Spend a moment and see if anything comes to you. There is never any need to force anything...just allow yourself to remain open by continuing to breathe easily."

92

Little Buddha Book Five

Okay, Ranger thought, I've gone this far, let's see what comes next.

The flash of insight startled him. It was as if a firecracker had gone off in the room, and a part of him wanted to open his eyes and jump up from his chair. But he didn't. He continued to sit, while concentrating on his breathing.

Suddenly he heard Dave's voice again and felt a hand on his forearm. He could tell instantly it was Jamie's, and it was warm and comforting.

Ranger opened his eyes to see relief rush across Dave's face.

"I thought I'd lost you for a moment," Dave said.

"What do you mean?", Ranger asked.

"Well, you seemed to disappear for a bit," Dave responded.

"Why, how long was I out?", Ranger asked, wondering what the big deal was.

"It's been forty-five minutes," Jamie answered.

Little Buddha Book Five

"No way," Ranger responded. "it couldn't have been more than five minutes!"

"Check your watch," she suggested.

Ranger glanced down, then back up at Jamie and Dave, "No way," he said again.

Jamie and Dave laughed, both amused and relieved to see Ranger seemed okay.

"Are you feeling comfortable enough to tell us what you experienced?", Dave asked.

"I can try," Ranger began, then continued, "I felt incredibly relaxed, more so than I've ever experienced. The event I imagined was from yesterday when I tried to punch Chase for pushing Jamie out of his way. It made me so angry. That's the word I chose…ANGER. Then you told me to go beneath the anger. I thought you were kind of nuts to suggest there was something else there, but there was. It was FEAR. All of a sudden, I realized that every time I've been afraid, I get angry, and I can't control it. It just boils over, and I explode."

Ranger sat back in his chair to catch his breathe. Once he was calm, he resumed speaking.

Little Buddha Book Five

"You wanted me to see if there was anything that could make my words disappear. I had no idea what you meant, so I just sat there. And after a moment I did know, and it blew me away. An image formed in my mind. It was a chain, a really heavy one and the links looked incredibly strong, as if they could never be broken. I knew each link represented something; I just couldn't figure out what."

"That's when it felt like a firecracker went off right next to me. I realized that every time I'm afraid, I react in the same way and another link gets added to the chain. Right now, the chain feels so long and strong and heavy. I feel held down by it. I realize I need a way to break the chain."

"Did you find a way?", Dave asked.

"Yes," Ranger said, "I think so. It's a simple way."

Jamie squeezed into the chair with Ranger and reached for his hand, taking it in hers.

The room felt immediately brighter, and Ranger sensed an internal shift happen inside him.

Little Buddha Book Five

"Surrender," was all he could manage to say.

"That's a great word," Jamie said, "it took me a long time before I discovered that word. You're amazing, Ranger."

No one, absolutely no one, had ever said anything like this to him before. Not in his whole life. And to have it come from the most beautiful girl in the world made it feel even better.

Dave broke in saying, "Ranger, what does surrender mean to you?"

"I think it means that for as far back as I can remember, I've been afraid of everything. I never felt sure about anything, and it seemed the only way to make it through my life was by being tough and anger is a big part of that."

"My father was a mean son of a…, sorry, but he was. And even though I hated how he acted; I began doing the exact same thing. And I suffered the exact same results. I was always in trouble. I didn't care. I actually wanted more trouble. I don't know how my mom could stand me. Maybe that's why she worked so much."

Little Buddha Book Five

Dave's voice was smooth and steady, showing no emotion, as he asked another question. "Can you share how this connects to the word, surrender?"

Ranger felt Jaime's head resting on his shoulder and it filled him with a sense of peace and contentment so deep he thought he would get lost in it.

"Surrender. It seems like it's the antidote to fear for me. I can see myself letting go as soon as I feel fear come to me. I give in, somehow allowing the fear to flow right into and out of me. I don't hold on to it, so it can't form a link to the chain."

"I don't see how it will actually work, but I have a definite sense that it will, once I know more.'"

Ranger stared down at Jamie's hand in his. "I know it's important and I want to understand better. I really want to change."

"You will," Jamie said, "you already have."

"Seriously, this was forty-five minutes?", Ranger asked, clearly still not believing it.

Little Buddha Book Five

"Yes, seriously," Dave said. "Well, I think this calls for some refreshments. What do you two think?"

"Absolutely," Jamie said, already getting out of the chair and heading upstairs.

Ranger and Dave followed.

After their snacks were finished, Ranger said, "I should probably be going. Thanks so much for a great time." He looked at Dave and extended his hand, "It was an amazing experience Professor, thanks again."

Dave smiled, took Ranger's hand, and held it while saying, "You are one special kid, and I should know!" He glanced at Jamie and reached out to tap the back of her left hand, then turned and went back downstairs.

"Let me walk you to the door," Jaime said, taking Ranger's arm in hers.

Once at the door Ranger faced Jamie and said, "Thank you for seeing me and giving me a chance. I really appreciate it."

To his surprise, Jamie leaned forward and kissed him very gently on his lips, then said,

Little Buddha Book Five

"See you again soon, daydreamer. Say 'hi' to your aunt for me."

Ranger felt his heart would explode with joy. The most beautiful girl in the world had just kissed him and he thought to himself, nobody will ever be able to make me move from here now.

He decided to go to the bakery and help his aunt out and was there when the flowers arrived.

"They're the most gorgeous flowers I've ever seen," Lilly said, seeing them come through the front door. "I wonder who they could be from?"

Ranger thought to himself, she'll never know because I didn't attach a card. However, it was then he noticed that it was the clerk he'd purchased the flowers from this morning who was carrying them in.

"Funny to see you here," the clerk said to Ranger.

"Do you two know each other?", Lilly asked in surprise.

Little Buddha Book Five

"Well, yes, we do. These flowers are from him…for you."

Lilly shifted so she could see Ranger's face, then started crying.

Ranger came over to her, hugged her and said, "You're the best aunt ever, thanks for letting me come here. I can feel my whole world changing. It all seems like a dream to me."

Lilly kissed Ranger on the cheek and hugged him tightly.

It was the second time he'd been kissed today, and he thought to himself, I could get used to this.

Little Buddha Book Five

revelations

Little Buddha Book Five

revelations

"You know," Sam said, "it's been a long time since we've done a project together and I was wondering if you'd like to do one soon."

Claire took Sam's hand in hers and responded, "That would be lovely Dad. Did you have something in mind?"

I still melted every time she called me Dad.

"Not exactly, I just had a feeling it was time. Is there something we could do through your home school?"

Claire paused for a minute considering, then said, "Yes, actually there is. One of my friends, Patricia, has been asking me if we could learn about a subject, she says has been fascinating her for a long time."

Sam seemed surprised by this, smiled, and asked, "What's the topic?'

"Well, Patricia wanted to learn more about the whole topic of death and dying. She feels she needs to reveal some truth, not only for herself, but to help others."

Little Buddha Book Five

"I didn't expect that," Sam responded, "have many people she knows died? Is that what's motivating her?"

"She has, but I think it's deeper than that. She sees the world through a different lens than most other people. I think you'll really like her."

"I'd love to meet her. When would you like to get started?"

"I'll call her later and see what her schedule is. What's yours like?"

Sam went to the kitchen and grabbed the family calendar.

Claire grinned at him, "You're so old school. You know you can put your calendar on your cell phone, don't you?"

"I did," Sam responded, "I have a photo of my calendar pages on it. But I like paper, so I still gravitate to the physical calendar."

Laughing, Claire said, "You're a riot. When are you planning on joining this century?"

"Eventually, I guess," Sam answered. "Anyway, I'm free every morning this week, so

Little Buddha Book Five

the two of you can choose what works best for you and let me know, okay?"

"Sounds good to me old-timer," Claire responded teasingly. She began walking away toward her bedroom, then turned back, "You know I love you, don't you?"

"I do, and it's one of the two best feelings in the world."

"I hope I'm the other best feeling," Janine yelled from down the hall, coming into view a moment later.

"You definitely are, my love," Sam answered, "and may I say how lovely you look. Being pregnant certainly becomes you. And think, in another three months, I'll have three best feelings in my life."

"How nice of you to say, Sam," Janine responded, coming across the living room to hug and kiss him good morning.

"What are you two up to?"

Sam leaned forward for a second kiss and answered, "Claire is going to call one of her home school buddies, Patricia, about the three of us working on a project together."

"That sounds interesting. Speaking of interesting, did I mention that I got a call from June yesterday?"

"No, how is she?"

"She's great and so is Gus. What she wanted to tell me was that her uncle Doug is going to be coming here to live. She and Gus have been researching Assisted Living facilities and found one they think he'll like."

"Oh, that's surprising to me. I thought the plan had been for Doug to live with them."

Janine nodded, "It was, but Doug says he needs a lot of help and thought it would be best for everyone if he was in a facility where there were trained staff around all of the time."

"That's probably for the best, especially since June and Gus travel so much. When is he coming?"

"Not for a few weeks. There's a lot to arrange first."

Little Buddha Book Five

"Does June need any help?", Sam asked.

"She says not at present, but once he's here, she could use a hand with moving him in."

"Absolutely, I'd be happy to see him and help with whatever they need."

Janine smiled, "That's what I told her. I thought I could speak directly for you on this one."

Janine circled her arms around Sam as best she could and gave him another kiss. Sam accepted the kiss and as he pulled back, kissed two of his fingers and touched them to Janine's pregnant belly saying, "There's one for you too baby."

Ranger's cell phone rang, and he reached to pick it up. Seeing the number displayed, he hit decline and went back to reading. He hadn't read a book for enjoyment since he was a kid, but Jamie had suggested one, so he decided to give it a try. To his surprise, he really liked it. The book was called, Alas, Babylon by Pat Frank and was about folks struggling to survive the aftermath of a nuclear explosion. It was really captivating.

Little Buddha Book Five

His phone rang again. He knew the caller
would never stop, so he decided to get it over
with.

"What do you want?", he said angerly.

"What I want is for you to get back here, so we
can finish what we started," a male voice shot
back.

"I told you already, I'm staying here. I'm not
coming back, probably never will. So, stop
calling me," Ranger said, about to hang up.

"If you don't come here, maybe I'll have to
come there. You still owe me, man. And it's
not chump change and you know it."

Ranger paused considering. He didn't want
Freddy coming to see him in his new home.
He'd wreck everything, but he didn't have the
money he owed him.

"Can you give me some time to get it together?
I'm working for my aunt, and I swear I'll pay
you back. You know I'm good for it."

The words came out sounding too pleadingly,
Freddy wouldn't respect that.

Little Buddha Book Five

"Yeah, right. Does your auntie pay you five hundred a day, dude?", Freddy asked, goading Ranger. "I don't think so. You remember the amount don't you…it's five large and a not a penny less. You know I'm not a patient man, so you decide. You've got three days. If I don't get my money by then, I'm coming to you. And, before I hang up, remind me, doesn't your aunt run a bakery? She must have cash laying around, right?"

Freddy let that sink in and ended by saying, "Three days!", then hung up.

Ranger picked up the book and threw it across the room, watching it hit a lamp, almost knocking it onto the floor.

A moment later his cell phone rang again. Instinctively, he answered it, yelling into it in a loud, harsh voice, "What do you want now!"

There was no response, just silence and Ranger quickly looked to see who the caller was. It was Jamie and he knew instantly this was bad.

"Wait, I'm sorry, I didn't know it was you, Jamie." His words came in a rush.

Little Buddha Book Five

After a long pause, Jamie spoke, "What's wrong Ranger? Who did you think was calling you?"

Right to the point, he thought.

"Please Ranger, you can tell me. The truth is always better out in the open. Truth and trust go together."

Jamie's voice was even, and he felt no anger in it, only expectation. He knew that right now was a turning point. If he lied, she'd let him go. She'd still be nice to him, but whatever friendship they were building would be lost.

"I'm in trouble, Jaime. Big trouble. I owe someone five thousand dollars."

The words had tumbled out of him and every second he had to wait for her response felt like a year. He expected her to give him a hard time or to ask a bunch of questions. He thought she'd be upset or tell him she didn't want to see him anymore, but she did none of these things.

"I want to help you. Can you come over right now so we can work this out?"

Little Buddha Book Five

Ranger closed his eyes, shocked to his core, that this beautiful person was in his life and was willing to listen and help him. What alternate reality had he stepped into by coming here?

Twenty minutes later he rang Jamie's doorbell. She opened the door, reached out her hand and took his, then led him into her living room and they sat together on the couch.

"So, tell me, how did this happen?", Jamie asked.

Ranger couldn't detect any judgement in her voice.

"I got in with the wrong crowd. I needed someone who understood me and at first a guy named Freddy seemed cool. A little rough around the edges, but so was I. I began with simple stuff, then he worked me up to bigger things, like stealing cars. He paid me a lot of money and I felt a part of something, maybe for the first time in my life."

Ranger paused to watch Jamie's facial expressions as they changed.

"Are you mad at me?", he asked.

"No, I try not to get angry until I know a whole situation."

"Okay, here's the story. I knew stealing cars was bad, but I also knew they were probably insured, so who was I really hurting and if I didn't do it, they would have beaten me up really bad. You don't know these guys, they never take 'no' for an answer."

"Well, one day I saw a beautiful new BMW sitting at the curb. Freddy told me to boost a high-end car and get it to him quick, so I decided I'd take it. Getting in was a bit of a problem, but I managed it. I started the car up and began driving away when I heard a noise in the backseat. I checked the rear-view mirror and there was a baby in a car seat looking at me."

"Taking a car was one thing, but kidnapping a baby was another. I couldn't do that, so I drove around the block, thinking I would just park back in the same space. The problem was that when I got there, someone else was already in it. Then, unbelievably, the woman who owned the car came out of the building, saw me in her car and started screaming at the top of her lungs. She reached for her cell phone, probably to call the police, so I put the car in

111

'park', got out and ran away. I thought my heart was going to burst out of my chest."

Jamie listened patiently to Ranger's story and held his hand, thinking to herself how different everyone's life is.

"What happened next?", she asked.

"I went home to hide out," Ranger answered, "and the next day I came here. I knew Freddy would find me and want his money. Of course, it's not really 'his' money, but that car would have brought him five thousand dollars, and the way he sees it, I owe him. He won't let it go until I pay him everything and if I don't, he'll come here and wreck everything. You don't know him like I do, he could even hurt my mom or my aunt, just to get to me."

Ranger sat with his head down, exhausted by telling his story and worried about Jaime's reaction and wondering how he was going to get out of this mess. He raised his head and faced Jamie.

"Are you mad at me now?", he asked.

"No," Jamie responded, "I'm not angry. Surprised and curious, but not angry."

Little Buddha Book Five

Confused, Ranger followed up, "What do you mean?"

"Well, you know I read a lot and I've come across stories about gangs, so I get why you did what you did. And I'm very glad you drew the line where you did and tried to return the car and walk away. I understand the pressure you were under and how it all seems too much to figure out. What I'm surprised and curious about is why you don't see the obvious solution."

Ranger thought to himself, if there's an obvious solution here, he certainly did not see it.

"What do you mean, what solution?"

"I loan you the money and you can pay me back from the money you earn at the bakery."

She said this so matter-of-factly, like of course kids their age all had big bank accounts.

"And where are you going to get the funds to loan me five grand?", Ranger asked incredulously.

Little Buddha Book Five

"From my savings account. I've been writing children's books in Braille for a couple of years now and have a balance of about eight thousand dollars. I'll loan you the five you need, and you can pay me back over time."

Ranger stared, open mouthed, but couldn't manage to speak. He was trying to let this sink in, and it was too much for him. She wasn't mad at him, didn't hold him accountable for his illegal actions, offered a solution to his problem and seemed genuinely happy to help him. This must be what heaven feels like, to be loved regardless of the dumb stuff you did.

He wondered again for maybe the hundredth time how he got this lucky.

"Ranger," Jamie prompted, "what do you think?"

"I think you are one incredible person. We only met a couple of days ago and you're willing to loan me five thousand dollars of your own money to help me out of a jam, a stupid jam I got myself into. Who are you?"

"I am someone who cares about you," she responded.

114

"Okay, let's say you really want to help me, and you can get the money, what are you going to tell your dad?", Ranger asked expectantly.

"I will tell him the truth, like I always do. You see, Ranger, that's what our relationship is based on- truth and honesty. Not parts of the truth, the whole truth. If I don't live like that every other part of me is filed with cracks. I don't want that, I want a firm foundation, one I can build my whole life on."

There was no way he was ready for this kind of honesty. He'd never been exposed to anyone like her, even his mom and aunt, as good as they were, they weren't like Jamie.

"Moment of truth," Jamie said, what do you want to do?"

Ranger hesitated a second, then said, "I'm in. And Jamie, thank you. You are the best person I've ever met, and I can't believe you care about me, especially after hearing all of this." A moment later he blurted out, "Why are you doing this for me?"

"Because I see who you really are, not who you appear to be."

Little Buddha Book Five

Floored, Ranger took both of Jamie's hands in his, brought them to his lips and kissed them gently.

"Okay," Jamie said, "let's go tell my father."

The doorbell rang and surprisingly I was the first to answer it. Usually, Claire beat me to it. I assumed there must be a reason why she allowed me to be the greeter.

I opened the door and discovered a diminutive young girl standing before me. She had pigtails in her hair and was wearing a very colorful outfit, accompanied by what I'd have to say was 'bling'.

She gazed up at me and spoke.

"You must be Sam, it's really great to meet you. Claire talks about you all of the time and I think we're going to be very close friends one day. How about we start today?"

All of this came out in what seemed like one breath.

116

I looked at her and responded, "Sure, let's start today. You must be Patricia, it's nice to meet you too."

"Yes, I'm Patricia, but my closest friends call me P, so since we're going to be close, you can call me P right now."

What an interesting young woman. I felt somehow that I had to change my description of her from girl to woman.

"Well, please come in P. I'm sure Claire will be here any second."

As I said this, I felt a tap on my shoulder, "I'm right behind you Dad."

Claire slipped past me and hugged P, then took her hand and the two of them glided by me into the living room.

"Come on, see if you can catch up Dad," P said.

It was a rare thing in my life to feel so instantly connected to another person. Maybe it was true what Claire had told me, that she felt we'd really get along well.

117

Little Buddha Book Five

I followed them into the living room and sat opposite them in my usual chair. I stared at them, and they broke out laughing.

"I didn't realize you'd be so serious," P announced.

"Me, serious," I returned, "you must have me confused with someone else." I said this while sticking my tongue out at her.

"There, you see, I told you," Claire said, while grinning, "he's right up your alley."

P elbowed Claire and winked.

"Okay you two, what's this all about?"

Claire nodded to P and she said, "Claire bet me that you would make some kind of face, if I egged you on and now she's won the bet."

"What's the prize for winning?", I asked.

P responded, "Can't tell you yet. It's some kind of favor I owe Claire. Sort of a 'yet to be determined' thing."

Little Buddha Book Five

"So, P, what's the project you wanted to pursue?", I asked, shifting our conversation a bit.

"Well, I want to know lots of things. Most of them relate to death and dying, not the morbid stuff, but how they fit into the cycle of life. I know they are not the end that others seem to think they are. They're just a part of a whole continuous process."

She paused for a second, then went on, "I want to know how it all works."

I sat back and pondered for a moment before finally responding, "I think we need another team member."

Claire instantly knew what I meant but waited for Patricia to ask.

"Like who?"

"It's going to take me a few minutes to explain, but I think when I'm finished, you're going to be excited to meet her."

"You mean she's here at the house?", P asked, warming immediately to the idea.

"Yes, she's always here. Would you like me to introduce you?"

P delightedly responded, "Oh yes, very much so, thank you. What's her name?"

"Lia," I answered.

"Is this the Lia, you've told me about?", P said, addressing Claire.

"It is."

They both turned to me and waited.

"Lia is always present for everyone if we want to talk with her. We can ask any question and she will answer us. The only time we can't hear her is when there's too much going on inside our heads. But when we breathe slowly, calming ourselves and become quiet, we are able to hear her. It's not that she 'comes' to us, because she is always present, we just aren't usually aware of this."

I waited and noticed P's facial expressions change.

"Sam, that sounds wonderful, can I meet her right now?"

Little Buddha Book Five

I nodded yes and smiled.

"How about I lead us in a guided meditation and once you feel at peace, simply invite Lia into your heart. Once you feel her presence, ask whatever you've been waiting to know. When your conversation feels complete, you can slowly return to your waking state. Does the sound okay to you?"

"More than okay, that sounds wonderful. Are you sure it will work for me?", P asked, hoping for some reassurance.

"Yes, I am. I've been talking with her for some time now and she always comes to fill my heart."

"Sam, please lead the way."

As I began the meditation, I sensed P relaxing immediately. I felt Lia's presence and slipped into my own conversation, releasing any need to guide P further.

About a half hour later I emerged from the depth of my meditation and conversation to find Claire and P sitting quietly, with their eyes closed. They looked like a pair of angels to me, and I was filled with a deep sense of love for them.

Janine came into the room, saw the three of us, waved to me and went back down the hall toward our bedroom.

A few minutes later, Claire, then P opened their eyes, saw me, and smiled. They both looked as though they'd been bathed in white light and seemed almost luminescent.

"Wow, that was…I don't have the right words…beyond magnificent," P said, stammering. "Lia is so beautiful, and she told me everything I wanted to know. How life starts and ends in heaven, which she referred to as the ocean of bliss. She told me everything begins and ends with free will, that each of us has unlimited choices, with no restrictions. That earth is a place we choose to come to create and experience whatever we decide, but that while we're here we often don't understand, because we've shifted our frame of reference from heaven to earth." P then added, "She told me we don't remember the truth."

Little Buddha Book Five

P closed her eyes and breathed in and out a few times, while Claire and I waited to see if she'd continue. A moment later she did.

"Lia explained that there is a ceremony held before we leave the ocean of bliss, It prepares us to transition from knowing everything to knowing and remembering almost nothing. She said we come to earth as sort of blank slates, so that we can experience fully what earth life has to offer, which is what she called 'duality'. In heaven you know everything there is to know. There is no question you do not already know the answer to. What you can't do in heaven is to 'experience' a thing you already know. She said that many essences decide to leave the ocean of bliss for a while and come to earth to create and experience the freedom to choose. Each of us is an essence, unique and special and a part of the one love that is heaven."

"She told me that each of us has a spiritual blueprint, which we created in heaven. It's sort of a guide to our life here on earth. We can change it, because we always have free will, but we mostly follow it because that's what we decided in heaven.

Little Buddha Book Five

P closed her eyes again and took several long, slow, deep breaths, seeming to need to replenish her energy.

Claire and I sat watching her with rapt attention.

"Lia said that birth was our entry into earth world and death was our exit back into the ocean of bliss. She also told me that we can 'return' to heaven in other ways by remembering the 'truth'. I didn't understand what she meant, so she explained that one of our earth choices is what she referred to as 'waking up' and remembering the truth, that our home is heaven, and that earth is a part of our chosen journey. Earth can be a beautiful playground, but she encouraged me to think of it not as a destination, because when our physical life ends, our heavenly life continues. As we breathe out our last earthly breath, we breathe in our first heavenly breath and return home."

P beamed at us, got up, came over to me, took my hands and pulled me up to my feet, then hugged me tightly and began to softly cry.

Little Buddha Book Five

"Sam, I can't thank you enough for introducing me to Lia. She's already changed my life and I am so happy. Thank you."

P held me for a long time. Claire eventually came and joined us, and our vibrational frequency soared.

I wondered again, for perhaps the millionth time, how I got to be so lucky to be here with these divine beings.

Little Buddha Book Five

Little Buddha Book Five

joy

Little Buddha Book Five

joy

"Are you ready to go," I heard Janine call from down the hall, "our appointment is in twenty minutes."

Claire and I came from different directions and met Janine by the front door, then went down the walkway toward our car. The gorgeous scent of our new family trailed behind us. Ever since we first knew that Janine was pregnant, the scents we'd each chosen and dabbed on our front door had changed. None of us could explain it, but we all knew it had. Just another of the miracles that happened when we were together.

Once in the exam room, the technician squirted goop on Janine's belly, placed the monitoring wand against her skin and began moving it around. An image appeared with astonishing clarity. We saw the baby's heart beating and could even see her sucking a finger.

"Do you want to know the baby's sex?", the tech asked. The name tag on her uniform read Monica. She smiled and waited for our answer.

"I already know, "Janine responded.

Little Buddha Book Five

Monica appeared puzzled and said, "Oh, I'm sorry, have you already been told?"

Janine smiled at her, extended her hand, and touched Monica gently on the sleeve, "No, but she already told me quite a while ago." Janine said this so matter-of-factly that Monica just stared at her.

"What do you mean, 'she told you'," Monica asked, the surprise in her voice evident.

"I can hear her voice," Janine responded, then catching the look on Monica's face added, "not out loud of course, but from inside of me."

This didn't help explain anything to Monica, who repeated questioningly, "From inside of you?"

"Yes, she let me know she's coming to be with us, to be a part of our family and then she told me her name."

Caught up in the conversation, Monica again echoed Janine's words, "She told you her name?"

Janine responded with a simple, "Yes."

Little Buddha Book Five

"How is that possible?", Monica asked, having difficulty squeezing out the words.

"Everyone has their own voice and their own name if you're paying attention. That's really the key. If you're always thinking your own thoughts, you can't hear anyone else. But, if you slow down and become quiet, you can listen and hear what others have to say. You'd be surprised by how much you can learn about the world this way."

Monica sat back in her chair, the wand still in her hand, and appeared to be considering Janine's words.

"Do you mean that you got really quiet and listened to your baby and she told you she was a girl and also told you, her name? Is that truly possible?"

"Yes, exactly," Janine assured her, "being open to the world gives everyone freedom. You create space and all sorts of things are able to fill the openness. In my case, my beautiful baby girl came and spoke with me, not only her name, but other things as well."

Little Buddha Book Five

"No way," Monica exclaimed, "you're teasing me aren't you. This is a joke the staff put you up to, isn't it?"

Janine slid her hand down Monica's sleeve until she connected with her hand, then interlaced their fingers.

"Yes way," Janine said, "and no, I'm not teasing you. I'm speaking my truth. Look at me and see it in my eyes."

Monica looked and noticed Janine's uniquely beautiful eyes and was immediately convinced. Tears welled up and overflowed, running down her cheeks.

Claire placed a hand on Monica's back to steady her, while I watched, amazed by the transformation taking place in Monica.

"Can you teach me how to do this?", Monica asked, hope clearly written on her face.

"I can," Janine responded, "why don't we schedule a time to get together that's convenient for you."

"You're an angel," Monica exclaimed, adding, "can we really?"

Little Buddha Book Five

"Of course, I'd be happy to share what I know with you."

Janine asked me to give Monica one of her cards from her wallet. I handed it over and Monica smiled, saying, "Thank you so much."

On our way out of the exam room, Monica tugged on Janine's sleeve and pulled her back down the hall a short distance. Janine went willingly, almost like she was expecting it.

"Does anyone else know the baby's name?", she asked.

"No, just me for now. It's not time yet to tell others. We need time to get to know each other before everyone else becomes a part of her life."

A moment passed.

"Do you want to know your baby's name?", Janine asked.

"What?", Monica sputtered, "how did you know I'm pregnant, nobody knows."

"I just knew," Janine answered cryptically.

Little Buddha Book Five

Monica stood staring intently at Janine, unsure what to think. She could be guessing, but it sure didn't feel that way. She sensed that Janine could see the truth. Maybe she could tell her how to talk to her own baby. She certainly hoped so.

"Tomorrow's my day off. Can I come to your house sometime in the morning, so we can talk?"

Monica felt she was being extremely presumptuous to ask one of her patients to help like this, but she was desperate.

"Of course, you have my card with my address on it. Come whenever it's convenient for you. I'm around all morning and would welcome your company."

Monica's anxiety relaxed and she felt more hopeful than she had in a very long time.

Janine winked and added, "Maybe the four of us can have a nice conversation."

Monica reached out and hugged Janine, "I sure hope so."

Little Buddha Book Five

"I can't believe it. What a story. What's going to happen next?", Claire said into the phone.

Jamie answered, "Ranger confessed to Lilly, then called his mom and told her. He said they were both nice about it, but he could tell how disappointed they were in him."

"What did your dad say?"

"Nothing I would have expected. He totally surprised me. He told Ranger, as a younger man, he'd made his share of mistakes. Dad said the number of mistakes you make is unimportant, because it's about the number of good things you do in this world. That's what really matters."

Claire was impressed that Dave saw life that way and commented, "Wow, Jamie, that sounds very enlightened. What's Ranger going to do now?"

"It seems no one wants to involve the police in any way and nothing short of paying Freddy what he thinks he's owed will solve the problem, so Ranger is trying to make arrangements to give him his money."

"How is Ranger going to do that?'

Little Buddha Book Five

Jamie waited a long beat before answering, "Ranger doesn't want Freddy coming here but Freddy said he had 'business' in the area and was going to stop by tomorrow. I think he's doing that to let Ranger know how easy it is to reach him in case he doesn't deliver the money to him."

"Can I be there with Ranger when he pays the money to Freddy?", Claire asked.

Jamie couldn't hide her shock and alarm, "Why would you want to do that?"

"I have a feeling. It's really strong and I know something needs to happen. I just don't know what exactly."

"Your parents will never go for that. Sam would demand to accompany you and having two unexpected people show up might make Freddy react badly. I don't think it's a good idea."

Jamie sounded more anxious than Claire had ever heard her.

"Jamie, do you remember the fire?"

Little Buddha Book Five

Her response was instantaneous, "Yes, of course, why?"

"Do you remember what you said to me, when you knew I was running into your house as it was blazing?"

"Yes, I told you not to go, that it was too dangerous. I remember it like it was yesterday. Why are you asking me that?"

"Think for a second," Claire responded.

"You saved my cat, Schrodinger, but what's that got to do with Ranger and Freddy?"

"Because they both need something and I think I can help them get it," Claire answered. "Do you trust me?"

"Of course, with my life."

"How about with Ranger and Freddy's lives?"

Jamie was silent for a while and Claire left the space between them open.

"Yes, I trust you. I know you always do what's in your heart and there must be a good reason you want to be there. I'll ask Ranger to see what he thinks. Can I get back to you?"

"Sure, anytime, but there's a clock ticking on this if Freddy's coming tomorrow."

Monica rang the doorbell and waiting, while biting her lip. She knew it was a bad habit, but she couldn't help it.

The front door opened, and Janine stood there smiling at her. "Please come in, it's so nice to see you again."

"Thank you. I'm so sorry for intruding at your home."

"There is absolutely nothing for you to feel sorry about, you're very welcome here. Sam and Claire are both out, so we have the house to ourselves. Come with me."

Janine turned and led the way into the kitchen and asked, "Would you like a nice glass of cold water?"

Monica laughed, suspecting that Janine knew most coffees and teas are considered

137

questionable during pregnancy and said, "Yes, please."

They sat and settled in. Janine uncovered a container on the table and offered Monica a cookie, which she accepted.

"How far along are you?", Janine asked.

"Maybe two months, I'm not totally sure. Do you think that matters? I mean do you think my baby will still speak to me?"

Janine smiled, reached over, covered Monica's hand with her own and said, "Let's see, shall we?"

"You mean right now?"

"Yes, why not? You still want to try, right?"

"Oh yes, definitely. What do I have to do?"

"Relaxing is the first step. Why don't we move into the living room, it's much more comfortable."

They did, and once seated, Janine asked Monica to close her eyes and breathe slowly in and out, relaxing her body and mind.

Little Buddha Book Five

"Allow your body to choose its own rhythm, just go along with whatever feels safe."

Monica began to visibly relax and soon she sunk into a deep peaceful place.

Janine stopped speaking, knowing Monica was moving at her own pace and was releasing everything she'd been holding onto when she'd first arrived.

After a few minutes Monica was making a soft purring sound, not snoring, but breathing in a peaceful pattern.

"Now that you and your baby are in a safe space, allow yourself to reach out and ask what you want to know," Janine said encouragingly.

Monica felt as though she was drifting, flowing, weightless. It was the calmest she'd felt since she was a child.

The moment she connected with her own childhood; she heard a voice call out to her. A small, quiet voice.

"Momma, is that you?"

Little Buddha Book Five

Amazing! Was this really happening? Could this be true? She knew she wanted it to be, so maybe it was her desperate imagination.

"Momma, are you here with me?"

The voice again and certainly not her imagination.

Her words tumbled out, "Baby, yes, it's me. I'm here and I love you."

"Momma, I'm afraid!"

"Oh, baby, it will be okay. Don't worry. Momma is here with you."

"Momma, I'm not afraid for me. I'm afraid for you."

Shocked, Monica's breathing hitched a bit, "Why are you afraid for me, my sweet baby?"

The little voice, almost a whisper said, "Because you are afraid. I feel it."

"Don't worry baby, I'll be okay. Momma will be okay," Monica responded, trying to be reassuring.

Little Buddha Book Five

"Please Momma, let go, you're holding on too tightly."

Monica froze. She now understood what her baby was saying. She was holding on too tightly. She'd had two miscarriages and was worried she'd have another. She found herself constantly experiencing her whole body tightening, sometimes even going into spasms.

Her baby's voice was calming, "I'm okay. I'm fine and I'm coming to you. I tried twice before, but I couldn't come through, but I know I will this time, so let go of your worry and be happy."

Monica felt her heart burst. Could this conversation really be happening? Could she rely on this as truth? Was this the same baby she'd lost twice before? It was too far beyond anything she'd ever experienced. Way beyond."

"It is true," her baby's voice said. "I am coming to bring you joy and to remind you of that, that will be my name…Joy."

Monica began crying. Tears overflowed and streamed down her cheeks unchecked. She was the happiest she'd ever been in her whole life.

"Oh, thank you baby…thank you, Joy. I can't wait to see you, hold you, be with you. I love you so much."

"I love you too Momma."

Janine watched Monica closely and waited patiently for her to open her eyes. When she did, there was a beautiful shimmering light there. It was as if she was a different person from the one who'd entered her home an hour ago.

Monica raised her arms, reaching out to Janine, who came, knelt in front of her and hugged her warmly.

"Thank you so much. Words cannot say how grateful I am to you. You've changed my whole life."

Monica continued to sob for a few minutes more, hugged Janine a little harder then released her. Janine stood and returned to her chair, while Monica reached into her purse for some much-needed tissues.

They ended up talking for the next three hours, until Sam came home and the three of them had lunch together, greatly enjoying each other's company.

It took several long conversations, but in the end, everyone accepted Claire's request to be with Ranger for the money exchange.

"What time is he coming/", Claire asked.

"I'm supposed to meet him at the diner at ten. I'm really not sure how he's going to react when he sees you," Ranger responded anxiously.

"He'll probably be so scared that he'll turn and run the other way," Claire said teasingly. "Sort of the same way you reacted when you met me."

Ranger laughed and said, "You got that right. That was maybe the most confused I'd ever been. You totally threw me off my game."

"So cool, huh?", Claire said, elbowing Ranger in the ribs.

Little Buddha Book Five

Ten o'clock came and both Ranger and Claire watched the front door of the diner from their seat near the back. They didn't want to draw any attention to themselves and definitely didn't want a bunch of people overhearing their conversation.

"There he is," Ranger said, pointing to a massive, tattooed man entering the diner, "that's Freddy."

Freddy spotted Ranger and another person sitting together. It was a girl. What was she doing here? Sort of lame protection, he thought. What could she possibly do to him?

"Yo, idiot, who's the bitch, and why is she here?"

Before Ranger could respond, Claire stood and extended her hand, "My name is Claire and I'm really happy to meet you. You must be Freddy."

Surprised, Freddy actually shook Claire's hand, then eyed Ranger questioningly and said, "I asked you a question, What's she doing her?"

Little Buddha Book Five

"I can talk for myself Freddy, why don't you
ask me?"

She certainly had guts, he had to give her that.
No one on the street would dare speak to him
like this. He wondered why it didn't bother him,
but he had no answer.

"Okay, why are you here," he asked,
accentuating the word 'are'.

"I came to negotiate a deal," Claire answered.

Ranger began to speak, but Claire cut him off.

"I'm what you might call, his agent," pointing to
Ranger.

"His agent, that's hilarious. He doesn't need an
agent, he needs to give me my five thousand
dollars, that's what he needs to do!"

It was clear Freddy was losing his temper.

Ranger again tried to speak and again Claire
cut him off.

"Freddy," Claire said, reaching out and patting
his huge hand, "he's prepared to pay you

145

everything you think he owes you. Show him the envelope Ranger."

Ranger opened the flap and pulled the bills out slightly so Freddy could see them.

Claire continued, "But I have something better to offer you."

Better than five K," Freddy said, clearly suspicious. "What are you talking about?"

"Respect," Claire answered simply.

Freddy stared at her, wondering what she could possibly mean. "I already got respect bitch."

It was evident that Claire had touched a nerve. Ranger was about to speak, but Claire turned her head, smiled, and touched a finger to his lips.

"Shhh, I'm doing what agents do. They negotiate. There will be time for you to speak later, but for now, please be quiet."

Freddy couldn't help himself; he was impressed with this girl.

Little Buddha Book Five

"Do you really have respect Freddy? I mean, whose respect do you have?

Claire watched Freddy's face carefully.

"Do the other gangs respect you, or do they hate you? Do the folks you steal from respect you? How about the cops or your neighbors? What about the rest of your gang? Is it respect or are they biding their time, watching for their chance to take over?"

Claire's questions hung in the air between them.

She'd thought he might fight back, but he didn't.

"And now the question that really matters. Do you respect yourself?"

This question crashed down on Freddy, and he wondered why he was still listening to her. She was beautiful, for sure, but the way she was speaking to him…it confused and unsettled him.

"It's okay," Claire said, reaching over and placing a hand over his heart, "there's time to change and I'll help you, if you let me."

147

Little Buddha Book Five

Freddy allowed Claire to keep her hand where it was. It felt warm and comforting, like when his Grandma used to hold and rock him as a frightened child.

"Help me how?", he asked.

"By finding your way back to yourself. You've been gone a long time, but you can still be the man you wanted to be. There is still a pure heart inside you, right under my hand. I feel it beating. Can you feel it?"

Freddy closed his eyes and sat quietly.

"Yes, I can. I remember, I wanted to be a good man, but that was so long ago. I don't see how I can get it back. I've done too many bad things. Been mean to everyone. I can't see how anyone will ever forgive me and give me another chance."

"It all starts with you Freddy," Claire said, and while leaving her hand over his heart, she reached over and took one of his hands in hers.

"All forgiveness starts inside of you. Once you begin to forgive yourself, it opens up space for you to change. And once you change, others

148

will notice and there can be open space between you. Open space for you to apologize sincerely and ask for forgiveness, knowing it's up to them. You have only one part to play, to forgive yourself and be true to that. Everything else comes after that."

Freddy opened his eyes and gazed at Claire. Tears began to slowly flow, "I want that. Will you really help me? I mean, why should you? Why do you even care about me?"

"Because you are 'kin' to me. I see you. You have something special to offer to the world. You've been looking in the wrong places, but you always have a choice what to do next."

Claire paused, looked at Ranger and asked, "Are you willing to extend a loan to Freddy? Will you give him these five thousand dollars to help him get his life back?"

Ranger sat, dumbfounded by this extreme turn of events.

"What?", was all he could manage to say.

"Okay, here's my proposal", Claire said, turning from Ranger back to Freddy.

Little Buddha Book Five

"How about we make an agreement that Ranger loans you, Freddy, these five thousand dollars so you can make a new start." She continued, "Freddy, you leave everything behind and promise not to go home for six months."

Freddy started to object, but Claire shushed him, "I'm not finished yet."

"Freddy, I'll help you get a job and an apartment, and you agree to pay Ranger back a certain amount of money each month."

"Ranger, you agree to help Freddy find his way around town and use the money to pay Jamie back."

"I will also talk with my mom and plug you in to the Community center," Claire continued, while looking directly into Freddy's eyes.

"How does all of that sound to you both?"

The question lingered, while Ranger and Freddy sat thinking.

Freddy could not believe he came to her an angry man, expecting to hurt Ranger, and maybe his aunt's bakery and now he was being offered a whole new life. A life without all the hassles of keeping his place at the top of the food chain. A place where he could relax and maybe, just maybe, become the man he'd always wanted to be.

Ranger could not believe Claire had turned such a dangerous meeting into a place of redemption. She'd done it for him and now was offering the same to Freddy.

"Take it man, she's giving you a chance at a new start. She's for real. She's done the same thing for me. You absolutely will not regret it!"

Ranger was so emphatic that Freddy snapped out of his thoughts.

"I'm sorry I called you a bitch." Freddy said, looking directly at Claire, "because you are definitely an angel."

Claire nodded at him and smiled.

Her glow was more beautiful than anything he'd ever seen.

"Ranger, I'm sorry man, for everything I've ever done to you."

Little Buddha Book Five

Ranger sat back in his seat and relaxed, "Thanks Freddy. I understand now and it's okay. I forgive you."

Ranger could not believe he'd forgiven so quickly, but the truth was he knew how it felt not to be forgiven, and that made it so much easier for him to forgive others now.

"I accept," Freddy said, "and I won't let you down."

"Okay, our negotiation is now complete, How about we celebrate? They have the best milkshakes here and I especially like their double vanilla ones."

Little Buddha Book Five

new life

Little Buddha Book Five

new life

"Hi, I'm calling to see if I can come over for a minute. There's something I want to ask you," Claire said into her cell phone.

The response was offered in an excited tone, "Sure, when do you want to come?"

"How about right now? It won't take long because I'm outside your place," Claire answered, laughing.

"Yeah, okay, I see how it is. I'm not doing anything at the moment and don't start work for another hour. Come on up."

Claire opened the outside door and began climbing the enclosed stairway up to his garage apartment.

He poked his head out of the doorway at the top of the stairs and peered down at her saying, "What's the occasion?"

"I came to find out if it's true," She answered. "Have you really changed your name?"

He backed up and she entered his apartment. "Yeah, it's true. Freddy doesn't work for me anymore. I think I kind of used that name up. I needed a whole new name, you know, part of my change to a new life."

"Okay, I get it. So, who are you now?"

"Abe," he responded.

"Interesting choice, how did you come up with that?"

"Well, Jax, you know, the owner of the garage and my boss now, gave me a book to read about one of the dead presidents."

"You mean Abe Lincoln?", Claire said, unable to conceal a smile.

"That's the one, He's a pretty fascinating guy. He had a thing about integrity and folks called him 'Honest Abe', and that's what I want to be…honest. I've had my fill of lying and doing bad stuff. I want to change things up.

"Well Abe, it's really nice to meet you," Claire said, extending her hand.

Abe took Claire's soft, small, warm hand in his and shook it gently. "It's nice to meet you too."

Little Buddha Book Five

They smiled at each other, and Abe spoke, "You know Claire, I can't thank you enough for this second chance you've given me. I'm in the perfect place. Even the name of this garage makes me feel good. When Jax hired me and told me I could stay in the loft I was shocked. "

Abe pointed through the loft's front window toward the sign hanging from the building and said, "This is what it's all about."

Claire looked out and saw the sign which read, 'New Life Repairs' and thought to herself, nothing could have suited him better.

Abe radiated energy and enthusiasm. "I love working on cars. I've been doing it my whole life, so this was a perfect fit for me."

Abe paused, then asked, "How did you get him to hire me, knowing what you do about me?"

Claire stood back a little so she could tilt her head up and see Abe's face better. He was at lease a foot taller than her, and she wanted to make sure she could see his reaction.

"I had nothing to do with you getting this job my friend. That was all you."

156

Confused, Abe asked, "But you said you knew him, that he was looking for a good mechanic, that he hired a lot of Excon's and that at the moment he had an opening."

"Yes", Claire responded, "I did say all of that, but I never spoke to him directly about you."

"So, I did this on my own?", Abe asked, surprised at how easy it had been.

"Yes, like I said, it was all you. So, now that you know the truth, how do you feel?"

"Outstanding. I never even would have tried for this job if it hadn't been for your encouragement. Thanks Claire, you're the best. I mean it." Abe paused and asked, "Now what was it you wanted to ask me?"

"It's actually a favor for my mom. She's wondering if you could come by the Community Center and help her with a project. Are you interested?"

"What's the project?", Abe asked.

"No idea", Claire answered. "Does it matter?"

Little Buddha Book Five

Abe laughed and said, "Do you always get your way with everyone?"

"Is it a 'yes'?", Claire asked, laughing deeply, then reaching out to hug Abe.

"Okay, yeah, I'm in."

"Great, here's my mom's cell phone number. You can give her a call when you get off work to set up a time to meet."

Claire hugged Abe again and said, "Guess I've got to go, see you later."

"Move in day Unc", Gus said, "pushing Doug and his wheelchair through the wide opening at the Assisted Living facility.

"Nice to finally be here," Doug responded.

An attractive woman approached them and introduced herself, "Hi, I'm Jackie, it's wonderful to have you join us. You must be Doug."

"In the flesh," Doug said, smiling.

"Here, let me show you around."

Little Buddha Book Five

Jackie led Doug, June, Gus, and me through the whole building, pointing out the dining room, Rec room, OT and PT offices and the library/TV combination room.

"Down the hall, there's an Activities room and our administrative offices. We'll catch them in a bit. I'm wondering, do you have any questions I can help you with?"

"I was wondering which door would be best to use to bring Doug's belongings through," I asked.

"Sure, no problem, that's actually next on our tour."

Jackie continued and finally completed the tour, stopping at Doug's room.

"All of our rooms are private, so you have the space to yourself. We supply certain things, but you can use your own furnishings if you'd rather."

June asked, "Can we hang pictures and things on the wall?"

"Of course, we want you to think of this as your own personal living space," Jackie said,

159

directing her attention to Doug, while answering June's question.

I always liked it when someone made eye contact and spoke directly with an older person. It made them feel valued.

Jackie was certainly good at her job, but I suspected she also had a real heart for the older generation.

A few hours later Doug's room was arranged, and he pronounced it 'fit for occupation'. He had such a unique way of communicating and I really liked him a lot. I sensed he had an incredible story to tell. I'd have to find a way to spend more time with him.

"Hey, can you tell me how to find Janine?", Abe asked, what appeared to be a young girl who was setting up a display of Lego buildings.

"Sure, let me show you," she said, leading Abe to Janine's office. "Right there", she said, pointing.

"Thanks kid," Abe said.

Little Buddha Book Five

She stared at him. "I'm not a kid and I have a name. Do you want to know what it is?"
Abe looked at her more closely. Damn, he thought, she wasn't a kid. But she was so short, he'd just assumed it.

"Okay, sorry, yeah, I want to know what your name is," he said, filling the open space between them.

"Daphne."

"Thanks Daphne, for showing me the way to Janine's office."

"That's much better," Daphne stated. "See you around big guy." With that, she walked back toward the front of the building.

Wow, he thought, nobody here lets you get away with anything.

"Come on in," Janine called from her office.

Abe did so and was surprised to see her sitting on a huge blue ball at her desk.

"What's that?", he asked.

Little Buddha Book Five

"Oh, this is my desk chair. It doubles as an exercise ball. Quite comfortable actually. Do you want to give it a try?"

"Nah, I'd probably pop it I'm so heavy."

"I don't think so, and if you change your mind, you're welcome to try it later. You're probably wondering about the project I'd like your help with, right?"

"Claire said she didn't know, but I think she did, but didn't want to tell me."

Janine laughed. "She's a real character, isn't she?"

"You could say that. I've never met anyone like her. She's pretty much my favorite person in the world right now for helping me get myself square with folks," Abe said, choking up a little.

Janine smiled, touched Abe's shoulder, and said, "I would love some help setting up for our Lamaze class."

There are chairs to put out and mats and a lot of other stuff. Are you up for that?", Janine asked, while pointing at her pregnant belly. "Kind of difficult for me to bend down a lot."

Little Buddha Book Five

"Yeah, sure, anything for Claire's mom."

As Abe was finishing set up, expectant mothers started filing into the room. Each one had someone with them. Abe knew how Lamaze worked, since he'd been a coach for both of his sisters when they'd had their babies. It angered him when he thought about the deadbeat dads not showing up for them, and despite trying to turn over a new leaf, he still wanted to punch them in their faces.

Just then a petit pregnant woman carrying a shoulder bag came in and sat down. He saw that no one was with her. He also noticed how shy she seemed, taking the chair furthest from the rest of the group. She was not what he would call beautiful, but she had something better, a sort of 'glow'. He couldn't take his eyes off her. Strange, he thought, then wondered what her story was.

"That's Piper and she doesn't have a coach," Janine said, resting a hand on Abe's shoulder. "How much time do you have today?", she asked.

"It's my day off, so I've got all day. Why?"

Little Buddha Book Five

"I was wondering," Janine said grinning
broadly at him, "if you would be her coach, just
for today. It's really important that she have
one and I can't teach the class and coach her
at the same time. What do you say?"

"You're kidding, right?", Abe asked, clearly
surprised by the question.

"Nope, very serious," Janine responded, "it
would really help her out."

Abe looked over at Piper sitting by herself and
thought about his sisters, wondering how they
would have made it through without him."

"Yeah, I'll do it," he finally said.

"Wonderful, I'll introduce you."

It occurred to Abe that this might have been
the real reason he was here, but he let it go.
"Where did you get that beautiful map?", Doug
asked.

"I ordered it on-line", June answered. "I
measured your wall, searched, and ordered
the biggest one I could find. It fits perfectly.
What do you think?"

Little Buddha Book Five

Doug wheeled his chair back a bit to get a better look. "It's fantastic!", he exclaimed, "I love it."

June felt pleased by her uncle's reaction. "I'm not done yet, not by a long shot." She took a few more things out of a box she'd placed on his side table and held them up for him to see.

"Are those the post cards I sent you from my travels?", Doug asked, his eyes growing wider.

"Sure are," June said, handing one to Doug. "My plan is to tack the post cards to the edge of the map, then tie a string of yarn from the tack, stretching it to a pin, which I'll stick in the city or country where you mailed it from. I've only brought a few today, because I thought it would be fun to take our time. As I put one up, you can tell Gus and me the story that goes with it. How does that sound?"

"That sounds stupendous. What a great idea, What's the first one you've got there?", Doug said, asking Gus to hold up the post card.

"Norway," Gus answered.

Little Buddha Book Five

"Oh yeah, Norway, that one has a great story attached, Maybe you need to sit down for this," Doug said animatedly.

"Why isn't my car ready?", a man said hotly, while approaching Abe, who had his head under the car's hood.

Abe stepped back and peered around the raised hood to see a red-faced older man staring at him.

"That's my car your noggin is still hovering over, and it was supposed to be done YESTERDAY!"

The man's emphasis on the word, 'yesterday' alerted Abe to trouble ahead.

"My boss isn't here right now, and he just told me about your car this morning. I can't explain more than that. Sorry."

"Well sonny, sorry is not good enough. I got places I need to be, and I walked a good mile and a half to get her. Now what am I supposed to do?"

"Don't know what to tell you sir," Abe said, trying to defend himself.

Little Buddha Book Five

"Where's your stupid boss?", the man asked.

"Hey, look, don't go calling other people stupid," Abe responded, getting his back up now.

"And don't tell me what to do. I used to be the head of a company. If we didn't deliver to our customers, there would be hell to pay."

He approached Abe and stuck one of his fingers into the middle of Abe's chest, "What are you going to do about this, pal?"

Abe's anger surfaced further, and he swatted the man's hand away.

"How about I deck you right here, how would that be?"

The man, realizing for the first time that he was picking a fight with a guy twice his size, backed up a few steps.

"You do and it will be the last thing you ever do," the man said forcefully.

At that moment, Jax entered the garage.

Little Buddha Book Five

"Mr. Rogers, I'm so sorry about the delay with your car. The part took longer to get here than they promised, so Abe just got started this morning. I called and left you a message, but I guess you didn't get it in time. Let me give you a lift home and I'll call you as soon as it's ready. I'll also give you a discount on my original estimate. Does that sound fair?"

Mr. Rogers considered, then said, "Not good enough."

Is there something else I can do for you," Jax asked.

"Yes, you can make the ogre over there apologize to me," he said, pointing at Abe.

Jax looked at Abe and waited expectantly.

Abe glared at Mr. Rogers, but knowing his job was on the line, he said, "I'm sorry I lost my temper with you."

It was the best apology he could manage at the moment, and he hoped it would do.

"And…" Mr. Rogers said, demanding more from Abe.

Little Buddha Book Five

Abe tried to calm himself. An image of Claire came into his mind, It was of their first meeting where he'd been so hostile and yet she'd been so sweet and kind to him. He wondered if he could do something like that now.

Another moment passed before Abe reached out, extending his hand toward Mr. Rogers, and said, "I'm sorry for the trouble you've been caused by our delay, and I'll get this done as fast as I can. I hope you can forgive us."

Mr. Rogers softened and responded, "Well, okay then," While shaking Abe's hand.

Turning to Jax, he said, "I'll take a ride home now please."

Later when Jax returned, he walked over and tapped Abe on the shoulder and said, "Follow me, Abe."

Abe wondered if his new job was over already. He sure hoped not. He liked it here, especially since he got to work on cars and didn't usually have to deal with the public.

They sat at Jax desk. Abe noticed a small sign hanging on the wall. Someone had neatly printed a quote on it, It read, 'It does not require many words to speak the truth' and Abe could see it was from Chief Joseph of the Nez Perce tribe. He thought about it and liked it. He'd been thinking lately there was too much talking in the world. People seemed to like to hear themselves talking all the time. Maybe it would be better to use fewer words.

Jax began, "Look Abe, I have a lot of ornery customers. Many of them are like that because they're used to always getting their own way. They seem to think they have to throw their weight around to get what they want, so they'll bully anybody in their path."

"You see that chain?", pointing to a heavy length of chain hanging on the wall.

Abe shifted his gaze and looked at what Jax was pointing to and said, "Yep, I see it."

"Every link is important. Without each one, the chain wouldn't mean much and couldn't do its job. Life is like that if you understand what each link means."

Abe was hearing Jax words, but not exactly following his train of thought. He decided to wait for more.

Jax continued, "In this case, the first link is tolerance, the next is acceptance, followed by forgiveness and finally, awareness. When all four are present, the chain is very strong."

It was beginning to make some sense, but Abe felt he needed a lot more if he was going to understand Jax point.

"Let's take Mr. Rogers situation and your reaction. He was angry because he'd been promised something and we weren't delivering, so he became aggressive. Because you decided to take it personally, you responded defensively."

Abe nodded agreement but said nothing.

"There was another choice available to you…tolerance. When you don't take something personally, you're not invested in the outcome in the same way as you might otherwise be. You can exercise tolerance."

"Mr. Rogers reacted to you by becoming even more aggressive. He felt justified."

Jax looked at Abe for a few beats and asked, "Did you know what Mr. Rogers was doing?"

Little Buddha Book Five

"Yeah, he was trying to pick a fight with me," Abe said decisively.

"Yes, and you offered to give him one, didn't you?"

"Yes, I did," Abe simply said, acknowledging his actions.

"The second link in the chain is 'acceptance', which doesn't mean you approve of his behavior, but that you accept that it is happening and that there must be some reason for it."

"You usually don't know the cause, but allowing yourself to be drawn into his world means you lose control. One alternative is to accept Mr. Rogers exactly as he is, no matter what."

"Notice I'm not saying you agree with him or think he's right, just that you take him at face value, then move to the next link."

"Which is?", Abe asked, unable to remember Jax original explanation.

"Forgiveness, This is what provides freedom for everyone, if that's what you decide. When

172

you don't take what another says personally and you accept what is happening, you set yourself up to look deeper into the situation. In this case, Mr. Rogers was very upset. We don't know what's so important to him about getting his car back, but clearly there was something. If we accept that and forgive his actions, whether he asks for it or not, we're free to see beyond the anger. We're ready for the awareness link."

"I get this so far. What's the awareness link?"

"It's when we look beyond the surface. I think you would agree that Mr. Rogers aggression was over the top, but what you don't know, what you couldn't know without asking is, why?"

Jax paused, then went on, "When I was giving him a ride home, he told me he was supposed to be visiting his wife in the hospital and that she was counting on seeing him. The fact his car wasn't ready meant he couldn't be with and comfort her."

"I had no idea," Abe said, clearly now upset.

"Exactly," Jax said, "the awareness link is so important because without it we don't fully understand. That's why it's valuable to ask questions and listen carefully to what's being shared with us. You see how, if your response is intolerance, only aggression exists. If you lack acceptance, you'll always be thinking about how someone should be reacting, in your opinion. When you don't forgive, there is no space for understanding. And when you refocus and increase your awareness, you can discover what's below the surface, the place where all answers lie."

"I never thought about any of that, but it makes perfect sense to me now. I'm going to try that next time."

Abe looked directly at Jax and asked, "Is there going to be a 'next time', I mean do I still have a job?"

"Of course, you do great mechanical work and now we're going to make sure you do great awareness work."

Relieved, Abe stood and offered his hand to Jax, who took it and shook it saying, "We're going to make a great team."

Little Buddha Book Five

leaping

175

Little Buddha Book Five

leaping

"Mom," Claire called out, "where are you?"

"In the kitchen, my sweet," Janine responded, "making breakfast."

Claire made her way to the kitchen. As she arrived, she noticed how ready her mom looked for her baby to arrive. In another couple of weeks, she'd finally be an official 'big sister'. It was thrilling to think about, and she wondered, for at least the hundredth time, what her sister's name would be.

"How are you feeling?", Claire asked.

"Like I'm constantly glowing from the inside out. Carrying her reminds me so much of how I carried you. I felt so deeply connected and I already know the two of you are going to be such wonderful friends, as well as sisters."

Janine opened her arms wide and beckoned Claire into a hug, which she warmly accepted.

"I thought I'd get a little practice in before the big event," Claire announced.

Little Buddha Book Five

"Going to help out at Day Care again?", Janine asked.

"Yes, they asked me to come back. I love working with the kids, especially the older group, if you can call four-year-old's, older," Claire said, smiling brightly.

"Where's Dad?", Claire asked.

"He was up early and went for a walk on the beach and hasn't come back yet. He wants his head to be clear for his book group meeting later."

"His head to be clear?", Claire echoed, surprised by the choice of words. "What do you mean?"

"Well, what he told me last night was that he's introducing a topic of his own today and wasn't sure how it would be received."

"What's the topic?"

The back door suddenly opened, and Sam came in.

177

Little Buddha Book Five

"Why don't we ask him over breakfast," Janine responded. "Good morning, my love, did you have a nice walk?"

"Outstanding, look what I found," he exclaimed, "It's a nautilus, which seems to be perfectly split in half so you can see it's beautiful design."

As he said this, he hugged and kissed Claire, Janine, and the baby, "Good morning to you, my girls."

Claire hugged Sam back and asked, "So, some big doings at Book Club today?"

"News travels fast around here I see," Sam said, looking at Janine, then turned to Claire and added, "yes, I want to tell you about some body conversations I've been having lately. I'm not sure how it relates exactly to the book we're reading, but I'm constantly thinking I need to share this with them, so I'm trusting it's the right thing to do."

"Want to test it out on us first?", Claire offered.

"Why don't we fix our plates, then I'll tell you all about it," Sam responded.

Little Buddha Book Five

They all chose their favorite breakfast items, headed to the kitchen table, and began eating.

Finishing a bite, Sam began, "We're reading a Louis L'Amour story called, <u>The Last of the Breed</u>. It's about a US Air Force pilot who is forced down on Russian soil, put in a prison camp and eventually escapes. He has to make his way home to the US on foot. I loved it and they said they wanted to read an adventure book. It's surprising how much conversation it's created, most of which is about how each of us survives in our own worlds."

"Sounds very interesting", Janine commented, "maybe I'll read it after you're done with it."

"Me too," Claire added, "but how does your body conversation connect?"

"We decided that everyone would share one of their own 'survival skills' with the group and my body conversations have aided me enormously, so I thought it might be helpful for them to know, in case they wanted to try them."

Sam continued, "I want to share them with both of you too."

179

Little Buddha Book Five

Sam explained further, then it was time for Claire to head out to the Day Care Center.

"See you for lunch," she said, kissing the tops of their heads, grabbing her backpack, and singing happily to herself while going out through the front door.

The day care occupied three rooms at the Community Center, each with its own bathroom and a door to the outside. Through the large windows you could see the expansive playground and picnic area.

As usual it was very loud. Drop off time always was. Actually, there would be a ton of noise until 'rest time', when it happened later in the day.

Junior was the first to notice Claire. He squealed with delight and ran, jumping into her arms.

"Miss Claire, you here, I so happy."

Junior often left out words, but everyone always knew what he wanted.

Claire hugged him and set him back down on the floor. A line had formed, each child wanting their own turn to hug Claire hello, which always made her day.

"Good morning, my friends, how are you all today?", she asked.

Of course, they all spoke at the same time, in a raucous chorus. This was another of her favorite things. For some reason it reminded her of going to the symphony with her mom and Sam. Maybe because she could hear the sum total the children's voices, but she was also able to pick out individual voices, like she could with the instruments. Each one different and unique, but a part of the whole, much like all of life.

Her thoughts quickly focused in on something else and she became aware it was like hearing the truth. Truth has many voices, none more important than another. What was beautiful and essential, she realized, was how they made you feel.

"It's my turn," Abigail said, tugging on Claire's sleeve, demanding her attention.

"Of course, Abby, ready for your rocket ship launch?"

Little Buddha Book Five

Claire placed her hands at Abby's sides and quickly picked her up and held her as high as she could, while making rocket noises.

Abby howled with delight, "Zoom, zoom, zoom," she screamed, deafening Claire in the process.

"Class, it's circle time," Miss Jenny said, gathering the rowdy group together.

All of the kids ran to the brightly colored carpet and sat on their favorite spots.

Miss Jenny led them through their opening routine, which they all loved, especially getting to be the weather helper. It was clear that Miss Jenny loved and cared for each child in her class. She spoke to them in a way they instantly responded to, knowing they were safe and would be taken care of.

Later in the morning, Miss Jenny announced that it was time for art.

Claire stood up and started assembling the supplies the class would need. She placed sheets of printed white paper and large containers of colorful crayons on three desks.

Little Buddha Book Five

The children hummed with excitement. Art was their favorite time of the day, except for Kenny. He considered lunch to be the best. This fact was quickly confirmed by anyone looking at him because his was the biggest lunchbox.

Once everything was ready, Claire invited the kids to come over, take a seat and wait for her instructions.

Matty, the smallest kid in the class tugged on Miss Jenny's pants and said, "Can I have my special chair today?", pointing to one near the back of the classroom.

"Of course, sweetheart, Danny, our maintenance man fixed it last night, knowing you'd be here today. I'll bring it over for you."

Claire explained it was princess and prince day. She held up a sheet and pointed out the design on it. "As you can see, there is a beautiful castle, mountains, a river and a prince and princess."

She continued, "What I want you to know, is that you can color this any way you want to. Use whatever colors you like and do as much as you want."

Little Buddha Book Five

Hands began reaching for crayons and a barely contained pandemonium erupted.

Claire thought to herself, this had to be the best definition of 'joy' she'd ever seen.

After ten minutes everyone was still hard at work, except Lucy, who appeared deep in thought. Claire walked around the table and quietly looked over her shoulder. Lucy had finished only half of her picture. Claire looked more carefully and noticed that Lucy had begun coloring the sky, the mountains, and the river, but had stopped each one, leaving parts of them incomplete.

"Hi Lucy, may I see your picture," Claire asked softly. Lucy turned toward her with sad eyes and answered, "If you want to, but it's not very good."

Claire held the picture for a moment and felt she understood. "Why do you say that Lucy?"

"Because", she said, pointing to several spots where her coloring went over the lines, "I can't do it right. My dad says I have to color inside the lines, if I want it to look pretty."

"Can I tell you something?", Claire asked.

184

Little Buddha Book Five

"Okay," Lucy answered in a whisper.

"Everyone has their own idea of what is beautiful. Your dad has one, I have one and you have one. What's wonderful is we each get to choose for ourselves. If your dad were here, he could color, staying perfectly in the lines and his picture would make him happy."

Claire walked over to a counter, grabbed a piece of paper, and brought it back, then showed it to Lucy.

"Here's my picture. See here, I've used green for the sky. Have you ever seen a green sky?"

Lucy stared up at Claire, "Nope."

"Well, neither have I but that's the color I wanted to make it, so I did."

Claire pointed to her mountains, "You see right here? I couldn't stay within the lines, so I made the mountains blend in with the sky. And you know what, I like the way it looks."

Lucy said, "I do too Miss Claire."

"That's the wonderful think about art, you can do it whatever way you want. It doesn't matter what anyone else thinks. They are free to color or draw or paint whatever way they want to."

"Really?", Lucy asked.

"Really," Claire responded, "do you want to give your picture another chance?"

Lucy picked up a purple crayon and started coloring in the princess's hair and the surrounding area, not bothering to stay within the lines, all the while laughing.

Once the class ended and all of the kids left, Claire pulled on her backpack, said goodbye to the classroom teachers and headed out the door.

She checked her watch and realized Sam's book club would just have started. She decided to wander by and see how it was going.

His space was down the hall and to the right, which happened to be on her way out the front door. How convenient, she thought.

As she neared the open door, she heard several voices, which must have meant they hadn't formally started yet because Sam was pretty serious about only one person talking at a time. He wanted to make sure each person who spoke had everyone's undivided attention. One clear, easily identifiable voice spoke, "What I was saying was that we each have our own set of survival skills. They may be different. They probably are, and that's a very good thing, because we can learn from each other."

Silence from the group as they allowed Sam to continue.

"I wanted to share one of mine with you. It may take a moment to explain but it's fantastic and has become a very meaningful part of my life."

There was some chair movement, but no one spoke.

Claire decided to move down the hall and head home. She was so proud of Sam, 'Dad" now. He was really good with groups, no doubt because of his teaching background. And when he was heavily invested in a topic, his passion brought all of his words to life. She admired the way he integrated the group and encouraged everyone to participate. He always told her that everyone has a valuable point of view, and it was up to the listener to remain quiet enough to hear it. She knew he didn't just mean the surface noise. He meant stilling their own thoughts so they could truly absorb what others had to say.

Back in Sam's book club room he was giving folks a chance to settle in deeper, saying, "Every one of us holds keys to a beautiful life, for ourselves and for each other. One key I've discovered is having a dialogue with aspects of myself. I've come to realize there are five I can easily identify: physical, emotional, mental, spiritual and ego. Each one is necessary for me to experience my best life. When there is anger, frustration, or a lack of understanding within me, it represents discord and I suffer in some way. When I allow each aspect its own voice and truly listen, I can find ways to open myself for healing. When there is honest dialogue between each aspect, my awareness grows, and my way forward becomes clear."

I paused and spent a moment surveying each of their faces. Some appeared to be following me, while others seemed to be lost.

SS, as we referred to Sean Stanley, was very perceptive and asked a lot of great questions. Ones that always served to stimulate our group discussions and additional group questions. Since I'm a huge fan of questions and I always enjoy seeing where they will lead.

SS asked, "Can you give us an example that might make it easier to understand?"

"Great idea," I responded. "Here's one. Recently I decided it was important for me to have a conversation about my overall health and to figure out some ways to become more able to live a better life. I began by asking my physical self what it needed. My method is to quiet myself, usually starting with slowing my breathing, and once I'm calm, I open to hearing what my physical body has to say. By the way, I write everything down and use different pen colors to represent each aspect. My physical self is brown."

I collected my thoughts for a moment, then continued, "I waited patiently for a sign that my physical self was ready to communicate. In almost every case it does. It's only when my mind is too busy, or I haven't allowed enough time for a conversation that this doesn't work."

"In this particular case, our conversation began almost immediately, and I was surprised by both the intensity and depth of my physical voice. It told me it could not continue its job

189

without more support and attention. It also told me that I had ignored it for far too long and it was definitely time for some changes."

"I'll share with you that I was shocked. Then a question occurred to me. When I used the word, 'I', who exactly was I referring to?"

"This question generated a string of additional questions, all essentially asking the same thing, who is running this show…who is running my day-to-day life?"

"Sitting with that was very interesting and it created a conversation where I had to canvas each voice for their answers. What came out of this was a pretty comprehensive plan, which I continue to add to as more thoughts and ideas come to me."

"I loved the evolution of this conversation because it became clear that, in total, I am interested in a quality life span, not in the number of years I'll be here. My mind, heart, body, ego and spirit all had valuable things to contribute, and I ended up sensing a set of very clear directions to take."

Little Buddha Book Five

"Wow," SS responded, "that sounds pretty awesome. Can you give us a few pointers to follow?"

"Absolutely," I said, "but I'd like to schedule that for another time, because I want to hear what each of you prepared for today."

"I'd like to share with you some valuable skills I learned when I built my house," Tommy said. "It was a huge learning process. I'd always wanted to construct something and use as few power tools as possible. I also wanted to do most of it myself, sort of a construction meditation."

Tommy continued, "I brought a few pictures with me, so you could see it in different stages. It's one of the most rewarding experiences of my life, both because it filled me up spiritually, but also because my whole family comes there and we have a great time."

Beautiful pictures were passed around and appreciative words and nods were offered by all.

About an hour and a half later we'd made it around our circle. I felt full of wisdom, enthusiasm, and joy. I knew how deeply we'd reached inside ourselves and connected. These folks were now even more special to me.

Ranger knocked on Jamie and Dave's front door and waited for the sound of familiar footsteps.

The door swung open, and Jamie stood, backlit from the sun's rays coming through the large dining room window opposite. It left no doubt in Ranger's mind that she was an angel. His angel.

"Don't just stand there silly, come in," Jamie said, already sensing what was going on.

Ranger leaned forward and kissed her on the lips. A soft, gentle kiss.

Surprised, but also delighted, Jamie said, "That was nice, may I have another?"

Not waiting to see if she was serious, Ranger stepped closer to Jamie, placed his hands on either side of her face and kissed her again.

"Okay you two," Dave called from the kitchen

doorway, "Could we please table that stuff for later?"

Interesting word choice Ranger thought to himself, as he shifted to holding hands with Jamie, as they moved toward the kitchen.

Dave surprised Ranger by extending his hand for Ranger to shake.

"Good to see you again, are you ready for another adventure?"

The three had met a few times and had discovered there was a real chemistry between them. Today, they were going to follow up on their latest conversation and try a new experiment.

Dave began, "I'd like to see what happens when each of us focuses our energy and thoughts on transformation."

The way Dave said the word, 'transformation', stretching it out as he said it, seemed curious to Ranger.

"I've spent several hours experimenting with approaches to use to aid us in transforming and I'd like to share them with you. Are you ready?"

Dave had a very unique way of presenting his ideas. Ranger glanced at Jamie to see if her facial expression had changed. Nope, same beautiful, serene glow. Obviously, she was ready.

"Yes, sir. I'm a 'go'," Ranger said.

"To me, transformation means shifting from one state of being to another. What I'm going to suggest is that we each create an internal profile of what state we'd like to shift to."

Ranger couldn't help himself and thought about two different answers: from solid to liquid and from here to California. He struggled to suppress his laughter and focus his attention properly.

"The profile I'm talking about is this. I want each of you to think of 'being' something other than what you are. For example, create a new you; your sex, age, skin color, nationality, physical location, even the time period you're going to occupy."

"Once you've developed your profile, place yourself in a deep state of relaxation. Not sleep, but relaxed, calm, and peaceful, like we've been doing lately. When you get there, allow yourself to slip into your profile, like you're getting dressed in the morning, one piece at a time. If something doesn't fit exactly, change it until it does."

Dave looked at Jamie, then Ranger and completed his instructions. "There's no time limit, no chance for anything other than success and the enormous benefits awaiting us. Any questions before we begin?"

Jamie and I both said, "Nope, we're set to go."

"Happy travels kids, see you later,"

And with that each of them relaxed into a deep state of peace.

An alarm sound came into the room. It took a moment, but they recognized the siren sound of a passing firetruck in the distance. It was enough to rouse them and bring them back to the present moment.

The look on Dave's face was interesting to Ranger, but he couldn't identify it. He wondered what kind of look it was.

195

Little Buddha Book Five

"That was amazing, Dad. I immediately leaped into another realm, not at all like here on earth. I had no body and seemed to blend easily with anything I looked at. I didn't have eyes but could 'see' everything. It's hard to explain. I knew everything and felt a part of it. Wave after wave of happiness washed over me. I felt blissful, joyful. I didn't need or want anything. I felt surrounded by light and the light felt 'personal' somehow, like I'd been here before. I felt completely at home."

Jamie finished speaking but the power of her imagery lingered in the room.

"It felt like heaven to me," Jamie added. Her face glowed and her smile lit the room. "I can't wait to go back there."

Dave let Jamie soak in the experience for a few minutes, then asked, "Were you trying to transform into heaven?"

"Yes," Jamie answered, "That was my plan from the moment you first started to explain your idea."

"Wonderful," Dave exclaimed.

A moment later Dave turned toward Ranger
and asked, "What about you, my friend?"

"I was in the jungle, and it was very hot and
humid. There were tents set up in a clearing
and lots of people. I was laying on a stretcher.
Two men came over to me and lifted my
stretcher up and carried me into the biggest
tent. There were many people there banging
on drums and the noise level was deafening.
The men carried me to the middle of the tent
and set me down in front of a large brown
skinned man. He began chanting and poking a
fire that sat smoldering between us. He
reached down and scooped up an ember and
held it in his bare hands. He blew on it and
smoke poured off. As the ember continued to
smoke, he held it over me then placed it on me
over my heart. I couldn't believe that it didn't
burn or even hurt me. His chanting became
faster and louder, until he screamed a word I
didn't know and fell to the ground shaking."

Dave was staring at me intently and Jamie's
mouth was slightly open, as if she'd gasped.

"What happened next?", Jamie asked.

"I felt a strong physical sensation, like
something warm was spreading throughout my

197

body. My hands, feet and head began to sweat, and I became very thirsty."

"By now, the large brown skinned man was on his feet. He walked over to a huge bowl, dropped something in it and brought it back to where I lay, then poured it over me. It felt cold and refreshing. He repeated this three times, then picked something up off the ground, held it aloft, then placed it on my forehead."

"I felt so different. Everything seemed to be moving inside of me. I felt like I was getting stronger and stronger, and I wanted to get up."

"I sat up, but the man rested a hand on me, shook his head and held me in place. A woman nearby brought me something to drink. It tasted very strong; unlike anything I'd ever had before. It was so intensely bitter, I thought I might throw it up."

"After I'd finished the drink, the man took his hand away and helped me stand. I wobbled a bit at first but felt strong enough to begin walking slowly. I sensed I was completely restored to health and began to run around the tent. Everyone was cheering, clapping and then the drums began beating again."

Little Buddha Book Five

"I heard the siren outside and came back here. This was totally amazing."

Dave asked Ranger what profile he'd chosen.

"I wanted to know what a miracle felt like, Ranger responded.

Ranger and Jamie sat, still quite absorbed in their own unique and exquisite experiences. A few minutes later, Jamie asked, "So, Dad, what happened to you?"

"I wanted to know what compassion felt like, so my profile was to allow the experience to unfold in whatever way that could be created."

"And?", Jamie prompted.

"It's truly hard to describe. The best I can do is to say I merged with an energy field of some sort. I became part of a 'feeling'. Not a person, place, or thing. A feeling."

"It wasn't one thing, but a combination of things. It was a mix of love, caring, mindfulness, peace, and power. I know that sounds wild, but I felt them all. They shifted within me, and I had an overwhelming sense of…compassion for everyone and everything."

199

Little Buddha Book Five

"It was magnificent and now that I've been a part of that feeling, I recognize it lives within me and I want to let it out. To give it away to the world."

Ranger spoke, "Dave, I have to say, this was the most awesome experience yet. Can we do it again soon?"

"Of course, but let's sit with this for a few days first, okay?"

Ranger nodded, then added, "I have to go for a run now, I just have to!"

Jamie and Dave laughed in understanding.

Little Buddha Book Five

arrival

Little Buddha Book Five

arrival

"Are you sure you won't get in trouble with your boss?", Piper asked Abe.

"No, he said I could work later hours one day a week so I can keep coaching you," Abe responded.

Despite her initial concerns, she found Abe to be a great coach and she felt a definite friendship beginning to form. He was actually pretty funny and sweet, once you got to know him.

They'd had coffee together a few times. Well, he'd had coffee, she'd opted for sparkling water with a twist of lemon. He'd confessed his past life was filled with mistakes and that he was trying to change and get his life on track.

When he'd elaborated about a few of his biggest mistakes, she stopped him and pointed to her belly saying, "You're not the only one Abe, obviously I misunderstood my boyfriend's intentions. I'd call that a pretty big mistake. Please don't misunderstand me. I'm very happy I'm pregnant because I've always wanted to be a mom, and I'm going to be a great one, it's just that a baby needs a father too."

"Definitely," Abe said, "no kid should be without one."

Their conversations roamed all over and each seemed pleased to spend time together.

"You're a really good coach, Abe. I feel so comfortable with you. Are you sure you want to be with me in the delivery room and all?"

Piper was worried he was just doing this to please Janine for some reason.

"You bet, I'm in for all of it," he said, reaching out and tapping the back of her hand.

She wondered what that meant but didn't ask.

"Have you picked out a name yet?", Abe asked.

"I've been thinking about that for quite a while. I have a girl's name I like, but I'm undecided if the baby turns out to be a boy."

"Is it a secret?", Abe asked, curiosity spurring him on.

"Crystal", Piper responded. "I like the way it sounds, but I also like the image in my head of a beautiful rose colored multi-faceted crystal."

"I like it," Abe said, "that's a really nice choice."

"Do you have any suggestions if it's a boy?", Piper asked, wondering if Abe would play along.

"None at the moment, although a couple may come to me. I'll let you know."

Abe looked out of the coffee shop window, as if watching for someone.

"Are you seeing if your ride is here?", Piper questioned.

"Yeah, Mr. Rogers said he would pick me up around noon. We still have fifteen minutes, but sometimes he's early."

"How do you know him?"

"Funny you should ask. He's one of my most recent mistakes. He came into the repair shop in a terrible mood and was in my face from the moment we made eye contact. He riled me so much I threatened to deck him. If it hadn't been for Jax, I may have done it. The guy wouldn't stop pushing me really got me angry."

"What happened next?", Piper asked, already invested in his story.

"Jax, my boss, intervened, made me apologize, then drove Mr. Rogers home. When Jax got back, we went into his office, and he explained things to me. He let me know Mr. Rogers was under a lot of pressure. He was trying to get to see his wife at the hospital because she was sick. He said that under normal circumstances he never acted mean or aggressive, so he knew something was wrong. Jax also gave me some great advice about not taking things personally, accepting people for who they are, forgiving them, even if I don't agree with their behavior and paying better attention."

Piper was impressed with Jax approach and words of wisdom. She was sure she could use some of it for herself.

"What did he mean by, paying better attention?"

Little Buddha Book Five

"What Jax said was that I needed to improve my awareness. To try to understand as fully as I can any situation I experience."

Abe looked at Piper and again felt his connection to her and to her growing baby. He was wrong in his initial assessment, she was beautiful.

"It's so incredible how it turned out, because once I knew what Mr. Rogers was going through, I fixed his car and drove it to his house, so he could visit his wife. When I got there, I gave him a real apology and told him I was sorry his wife was sick and asked if there was anything I could do for him."

Abe shook his head from side to side and said, "He accepted my apology, shook my hand, and offered to drop me back at the repair shop on his way to the hospital. Ever since then we've kept in touch and even had dinner together once his wife came home. Her name is San. I don't know if it's short for something else but she's incredibly nice."

"So, you are friends with them?", Piper said, as a statement rather than a question.

Little Buddha Book Five

"Yes, I guess we are," Abe said, smiling to himself. "Oh, I almost forgot to tell you. Mr. Rogers told me this great story about two presents. Do you want to hear it? I think I have enough time to share it before he gets here."

"I do," Piper simply said.

"So, there was this man, and he was sitting on a park bench and a teenage girl ended up plopping down next to him. The girl looked at the two presents sitting next to the man and asked him who they were for. The man casually looked around, then directly at her and said, one of them is for you. The girl looked more carefully at the presents and noticed one was gorgeous. It had beautiful paper, a satiny ribbon and exquisite bow. It appeared to have been wrapped by an expert because she couldn't even find a hint of tape. The other present was wrapped in plain brown paper, like it had been a shopping bag at one time. It was folded poorly and badly taped. The girl wondered about the two presents, but even more so about the man. What was he up to? Why was he offering her one of the presents and why allow her to choose? She finally decided she didn't really have anything to lose and pointed at the gorgeous present. The man said, it's yours now, go ahead and open it,

207

which she did. Inside was a useless, beaten-up old Timex watch. Thanks, she said, sarcastically, then looked at the man's eyes. They were smiling and it made her curious. What's in the other present, she asked. We'll have to wait for the next person to come along he told her. She frowned and said, but I don't have any more time to wait, I've got to get to work. Oh, he asked, where do you work? A jewelry store a few blocks away, she responded. I have an idea, the man said, why don't you take it with you. She grinned and asked if he meant it. He said that he did, and she thanked him and walked away carrying it with her. When she got to the jewelry store, she put down her things, then opened it. Inside was a beautiful sparkling diamond and a note. She unfolded the note and read it, 'Inside each of us is a treasure, I hope you always find it so!' The girl hurried and found the owner and asked him to check the diamond out. He took it from her, squinted through his eye piece magnifier and said, it's superb and has fantastic clarity. Where did you get it? It was a present from someone. Is it valuable the girl asked? 'Very', the man said, he must be quite a good friend. The girl thought about the diamond, but found herself focused on the note, wondering if inside of her there was a valuable treasure."

Little Buddha Book Five

"That's mine," the young woman said
emphatically.

"According to you", the young man walking
next to her growled, "but I don't see it that way.

I watched the two from behind as they
continued walking and noticed their argument
heat up further.

"Of course, you wouldn't. You think everything
belongs to you. It must be nice," she
countered.

"Who has the sales receipt?", he asked.

"Just because you paid for it doesn't mean it
belongs to you. You gave it to me as a present
if you remember," she responded.

They stopped walking, stood, and faced each
other, both clearly upset and neither intending
to back down.

I recognized them now. They both came to my
book club occasionally.

The couple saw me and tried to hide their
argument by smiling and greeting me warmly.

Little Buddha Book Five

"Nice to see you, Sam," Maggie said.

"Sorry we haven't been coming recently," Brad added, "we've both been slammed at work."

"Great to see you too," I said, "and please don't feel you need to apologize to me. I'm just happy when you come. You both add so much to our group, and I love your insights about the books we read."

Maggie looked at Brad, then turned to me and said, "Can I ask you something?"

She'd found me to be perceptive and wondered what I would think about their argument.

Brad gave Maggie a look which clearly said that she was stepping over a line by including me.

I was reluctant to become directly involved, but I sensed I might be able to shed some light that could be helpful.

"Sure," I answered, "but only if you both agree."

Little Buddha Book Five

Brad still appeared apprehensive, but since I'd made any response on my part contingent on his approval, he felt it was okay and said, "Sure, go ahead."

Maggie opened by saying, "So, let's say we have a situation where we disagree and neither of us feels the other has a valid position. How would you go about giving us some advice?"

Well, I thought, that was pretty general, and more detail would certainly help, so I asked, "Can you be a little more specific? What are the two different opinions based on?"

Brad jumped in, "I guess you could say the essence of the topic is, ownership."

I nodded to him and looked at Maggie for confirmation.

"Agreed," she said.

"It's certainly an interesting concept and one I've struggled with a lot in my life. I used to believe very strongly that if I bought something, that I owned it. No one could take it away from me or, if they'd given it to me, they

Little Buddha Book Five

couldn't take it back from me, because now I owned it."

I paused to gauge their reactions. I was quite sure they didn't know I'd overheard some of their conversation. Since my statement covered both of their positions, I was curious to see what they'd say.

They looked at each other and seemed unsure of their next move.

Maggie broke the ice by telling me, "Brad seems to think that because he bought me something as a gift with 'his' money, that it still belongs to him." Maggie emphasized the word, 'his'.

"And she maintains that since I gave it to her, I don't have any further say in the matter," Brad said, continuing to advocate for his position.

"I think I understand your positions. What might be helpful is to explore where they came from. Brad, when you were a kid, did your parents buy you things?"

"Of course, they were really well off, so I got pretty much anything I wanted," he answered.

Little Buddha Book Five

"If you misbehaved or didn't meet all of their expectations, what happened?"

Brad facial expression shifted from anger to sadness, as he recalled his childhood. He lowered his head a bit and answered, "If I didn't do everything they wanted and do it when they wanted, they'd threaten to take away the things they'd given me that I most treasured."

Maggie reached out toward him and gently placed her hand on his arm.

"Not only did they threaten, but they executed their threats. After a while, I'd just go to my room and throw whatever it was they were threatening to take away into the hallway and close my door."

"That's awful, Brad. You never told me that before. I am so sorry."

Brad acknowledged Maggie's sympathy and quietly said, "I'm so sorry Maggie, is that the way I made you feel?"

She hugged him and when she pulled away said, "Kind of, yeah."

Little Buddha Book Five

"I'm going to try really hard to never do that again, okay babe?"

Maggie nodded 'yes' and after another moment said, "I think I realize something about my upbringing too."

"What is that?", I prompted.

"My parent rarely gave my sisters and me anything. They were both extremely selfish people. It wasn't until my sisters and I had jobs that we had some nice things. So, when I get a gift from someone, it means a lot to me. I guess I see it as a way they're telling me they love me."

She looked at Brad, then lowered her gaze. "When you told me you still owned the gift because you paid for it, the gift felt conditional, like there were strings attached. That's not the kind of love I want in my life."

Brad hugged Maggie hard and murmured, "I'm sorry," over and over again. "Please forgive me. I do love you. So much. I understand what's happening now- to both of us. Now that I get it, I can change. Maggie, I will change."

Little Buddha Book Five

Comforted, Maggie hugged Brad back and said, "I get it now too and I'm sorry for the way your parents treated you. We're going to have to do better when we're parents."

I watched, fascinated, that one simple question had opened all of this up for them to see clearly.

"Thank you, Sam," Maggie said, tears forming in the corners of her eyes.

"Yes, really, Sam, you're the best. I think we need to get our acts together and put work in its right place and carve out time to come back to your book club."

Maggie shook her head in agreement.

"I think you two did all of the heavy lifting to see past your obstacles and resolve whatever problem you were having. I do want to say one more thing. Over time I've come to realize none of us actually 'own' anything. At most, we are caretakers. Once we shift our mind from ownership to a heart of caretaking, everything becomes clearer. Part of our journey here on earth is recognizing and encouraging this shift. I think that's something both of you are going to become very good at."

215

Little Buddha Book Five

Maggie approached me and spread out her
arms and wrapped them around me in a divine
hug. When she let go, Brad stretched out his
hand and taking it, we had a bonding shake,
both knowing it would be the first of many.

A few days later I was washing the lunch
dishes while Janine dried and Claire loaded
the dishwasher.

"Oh," Janine said, leaning against the counter
for support. She set down the glass she was
drying and grabbed my arm. "Sam, I think my
water just broke."

Claire and I immediately looked at the floor.

"Yup," Claire said, "it sure did, time to go into
action." She guided Janine to the closest chair
and told her to stay put.

Looking at me, she said," Dish cloth down, dry
your hands, get your wallet, cell phone, car
keys and the 'go-bag' and meet us at the car."

Claire would have made an excellent drill
sergeant, giving orders and demanding
confidence.

"But," I started to say, before she cut me off.

Little Buddha Book Five

"Now, Dad, do it right now. I came really quick, so there's no time to waste. Move it!"

I did as I was told, grabbing our stuff, and heading out the front door.

Moments later, Janine, with Claire guiding and supporting her, stood by the front passenger door. Claire opened it and helped her mom in, adjusting the seat belt as quickly as she could. Once in the car, Claire barked out her next command, "Go Dad, hit it."

I did so and managed to get us to the hospital in under twelve minutes, better than any of my practice rounds.

Claire began helping Janine out of the car and yelled to me to get a wheelchair and let them know a pregnant mom was coming.

I ran off and was back in two minutes, pushing the wheelchair, followed by two nurses.

They took over for me and rushed us in through the emergency door. One nurse pulled me aside and said, "You have to check in. It's over there," pointing to a set of cubicles.

Little Buddha Book Five

Claire shouted to me, "I'll stay with mom. Come find us when you're done."

I provided all the information they wanted, including my health insurance ID card and Driver's license, even though I didn't know why they wanted it.

A few minutes later, I located the emergency room reception desk and asked where Janine was taken. A very nice receptionist gave me directions and I found Janine and Claire and several medical staff in an area separated by curtains.

"Good, you're here," Janine said, reaching out her hand to me.

"You're fully dilated," a nurse with scrubs announced, "we need to move you to the OR right now."

Janine said, "I want both of them to be with me," pointing to Claire and me. The tone of her voice must have immediately convinced the staff, so they handed us both scrubs to put on.

"This way," one of them said, helping me secure the top and middle ties, then pushing me down the hall.

218

Little Buddha Book Five

I made it as far as the operating room door
before I passed out on the floor. One nurse
checked my pulse, then headed off. A moment
later one of the ER nurses came over and
stayed with me.

Claire followed everyone into the OR and
stood next to Janine, holding her hand, and
reminding her to breathe like they'd practiced.

When I came to, the ER nurse was taking my
blood pressure and oxygen level.

"How do you feel?", she asked.

"Pretty lame for fainting," I told her, "but I feel
fine now. Can I still go be with my wife and
daughter? My baby is about to be born and I
want to be there."

"I'll go ask. Stay here, okay?"

"Yes, but please hurry."

About a minute later she returned and led me
into the operating room where Janine, Claire
and the medical staff were.

"Sorry," I said.

Little Buddha Book Five

"Never mind that," Claire said, "go around and hold mom's other hand."

I did as I was told. Between contractions, Janine asked, "Are you okay? What happened?"

"Passed out for the first time in my life," I answered, "but I'm good now. How are you doing?"

Janine let out a controlled roar and crushed my hand.

"Your baby is coming right now," Dr. Netter, the OB/GYN announced. "One more good push, okay. Now."

Janine screamed and pushed as hard as she could.

There was the piercing sound of crying the next moment and our baby was here.

Dr. Netter passed our baby to the nurse, who swaddled her.

"You have a beautiful baby girl, Janine."

Little Buddha Book Five

"We have a beautiful baby girl," Janine corrected.

Claire and I looked at Janine and we all began to laugh and cry at the same time.

The nurse finished her new baby procedures, then brought our daughter over and laid her on Janine's chest.

Janine hugged her gently and rocked her as best as she could.

"Welcome to the world, Brooke," she whispered. "It's so wonderful to finally meet you in person. You are so beautiful."

Holding her up a little, Janine said, "I'd like to introduce you to your father and sister."

Claire and I, still crying, said in unison, "Hello, beautiful baby Brooke."

After Janine had a few minutes with Brooke, she handed her to me. I cradled her against my chest and stared into her gorgeous blue eyes.

A few moments later, I handed Brooke to her anxiously awaiting sister.

Little Buddha Book Five

"Hello, Sis. We're going to be such good friends, I promise."

"Mom, Dad, did you notice anything?", Claire asked. "She smells exactly like the scent on our front door."

Janine leaned toward Brooke and said, "Wow, you're exactly right. She's certainly in the right place, isn't she."

"She sure is," I said.

questions for going deeper

Little Buddha Book Five

I want to offer you an opportunity to go deeper into the stories, so the following questions provide you an opportunity to explore. Hopefully this will be helpful for those who would like to spend some time in self-study or perhaps, for group study and discussion.

Chapter One Questions

Have you ever known who was on the phone before it rang? If so, how do you think that happened?

What do you believe happens to you moment after you die? Do you think there could be a place like Walt visited?

Were you surprised when the person told Walt they were 'home'? What do you think he meant?

Do you think you'll see people you know after you die?

What do you think the person meant by 'lateral time, especially about it being vertical rather than horizontal?

What mental state do you think coma patients are experiencing? Could it be a place where they are suspended, deciding whether they are coming back to earth or not?

Do you believe folks who 'die' are given a choice to return to earth?

Little Buddha Book Five

If you were in a coma for a long time, how do
you think it would be once you returned to
earth? Might you change the way you want to
live?

Do you believe you have free will, the ability to
choose for yourself? If so, does it exist even
after you die?

Do you think you'll have greater awareness
about your life after you die, like what
everything meant? Do you think you'll
understand, or would you like to change
things?

Chapter Two Questions

Has a stranger ever surprised you with an act of kindness, like Pat did for Sam?

Have you ever been visited by someone who died and felt their presence? If so, how do you account for that?

Do you think we all get a choice of whether to come back from death, perhaps to fulfill a mission of some sort?

Do you find Walt's decision to sell everything and move to be surprising?

If you were Walt's friend and he told you he was moving far away to be of service to 'his people', what might you have said to him?

What do you think of Walt's statement that he 'has a lot of breathing and centering and listening' to do in regard to his decisions?

Can you understand why Walt is no longer afraid of death? Does his experience effect the way you feel about death?

Do you ever question your beliefs and end up reexamining them? If so, what has happened?

Little Buddha Book Five

What do you think of Walt's thoughts about the aging process and how what he believes impacts what he experiences?

Do you agree with Walt's new awareness that every choice is available to us and that we get to decide?

What do you think of Walt's idea to meet in one year to review their lives and the decision they've made? Would you like to do that with your friends?

What do you think about 1) Lynn's belief to explore the idea about running out of time, 2) Walt's belief there's only so much one person can do and 3) Sam's whole idea of 'deserving'?

Chapter Three Questions

Do you have a friend like Sam you can count on to help you when you need it? Are you that kind of friend?

Is there someone special in your life, like Lilly is to Ranger?

Have you ever had to deal with someone like Ranger who is angry and defiant? What approach did you use, and did you have to try alternate approaches as well?

Are you surprised that Lilly trusts Lia and somehow knows everything will work out for Ranger?

How would you feel to be displaced, like Ranger, then be told you would be helping out baking, starting at 4:00am?

When you are frustrated, do you try to control things, like Carol did with Ranger?

Have you ever had to try to forge a positive relationship with someone who is defiant? What did you do that worked?

Little Buddha Book Five

What do you think about Lilly's faith in Lia and her belief it would result in a positive outcome for Ranger?

How much strength do you think it took for Lilly to deal with Ranger? If you were her, what would you have done?

Were you surprised that Claire was up and dressed and ready to help Sam find Ranger?

What did you think about Claire's idea to be the one to approach Ranger? What did you think she would say to him?

Did you like how Claire disarmed Ranger, confusing and intriguing him with her line of questions? How might you have felt if you were Ranger?

Do you believe what Claire told Ranger that, 'we're all each other's lifelines'?

Were you surprised that Claire was able to reach Ranger and that he accepted her invitation?

Chapter Four Questions

Have you ever blurted out a question or statement without thinking, like Ranger did about Jamie being blind? If so, how did it play out?

What do you think of Dave's 'night school' idea?

Do you understand Dave's frustration with not being able to share the vision he sees for the web of creation? Do you ever have difficulty capturing words to explain something important to you?

What do you think of Dave's vision of the web of creation? Did you try to imagine it along with the group? If so, what did you see?

Could you see the web expanding and contracting when you breathed in and out? How did it feel?

What do you think of Claire's description of her homeschool? Would you like to have gone to one when you were a student?

Little Buddha Book Five

Were you shocked that there were no grades in Claire's homeschool and that the focus was on learning and extending their knowledge?

Were you surprised that Jamie was able to block Ranger's attempted punch? What did you think of her explanation?

Do you agree with Jamie's assessment of violence?

What do you think of Jamie's suggestion that Ranger and Chase use night school to explore the motives for their actions in order to gain some valuable insight?

Little Buddha Book Five

Chapter Five Questions

What do you think about Jamie's statement to Ranger, about carrying around our mistakes and how much they weigh? Do you carry your mistakes with you?

Do you remember the first time when someone important to you said that they liked/loved you? How did it feel?

Like Ranger, do you often wish you knew more than you do about something? How could you change that?

Have you ever done something impulsively for someone? If so, how did it work out?

Do you remember your first hug from someone other than your family? How did it feel?

What does a handshake mean to you? Do you have a good one? Can you tell something about someone else by their handshake, like Dave did with Ranger?

Would you have chosen to be a part of an experiment that Dave created? If not, what reservation would you have had?

Little Buddha Book Five

If you were to do the experiment with Dave, Jamie, and Ranger, what experience would you choose? What one word would characterize it and what deeper word would be beneath the surface?

Do you have a chain, like Ranger has? Is yours based on fear too? If not, what is yours made of?

What are your feelings about the word, 'surrender'? Can you use surrender as a way for anything that troubles you to flow into, through and out of you?

Has anyone ever given you a chance you felt you didn't deserve? Is this something you could do?

Has anyone ever given you flowers and surprised you? Have you done this for someone else? How did it feel?

Chapter Six Questions

If you were going to do a homeschool project with Claire, what would you choose?

Have you ever read, <u>Alas Babylon</u> by Pat Frank? If not, I recommend it, it's a great read.

Have you ever owed money to another person, like a family member or friend? How did it make you feel?

Do you agree with Jamie that truth and trust go together and that truth is always better out in the open? Why do you feel the way you do?

Were you surprised that Jamie would want to help Ranger figure things out about his owing five thousand dollars to Freddy? What would you have said to him?

How do you feel about Jamie's statement to Ranger about building her life on a firm foundation?

What did you think when Jamie responded to Ranger's question about why she was helping him, and she said, "because I see who you really are, not who you appear to be"?

Little Buddha Book Five

Have you ever met someone you immediately clicked with? Did your relationship last a long time?

What do you think about what P heard from Lia about heaven and earth, especially the part about the ceremony?

Were you surprised by any of the things Lia told P? Do they feel true to you?

What do you think about each of us having our own spiritual blueprint? And what do you think about its connection to 'free will'?

Do you believe that once we take our last breath on earth that our next breathe will be taken in heaven?

Chapter Seven Questions

Do you think it is possible for an unborn baby to communicate with its mother, the way Janine said hers did? Has this happened to you?

Have you ever experienced someone like Janine, who spoke her truth which conflicted with all you'd ever been taught BUT you believed them? If so, what was that like for you?

If you were Monica, would you have accepted Janine's invitation to talk more about inner communication?

At the end of the exam appointment, Monica hugged Janine, sensing a deep connection. Do you ever hug someone or wish you could because you feel a deep connection? If so, how does that feel to you?

What do you think of Dave's reaction to what Ranger did, saying the number of mistakes you make are unimportant because it's about the number of good things you do in this world that matters? Do you agree with Dave?

Little Buddha Book Five

Were you surprised that Claire wanted to be at the meeting between Ranger and Freddy? Why do you think she wanted to be there?

Jamie took some convincing by Claire to agree to support her decision. What do you think convinced her?

What do you think about Janine's process for Monica being able to speak to her unborn baby? Do you believe it's possible? Why?

How did you feel during Monica's conversation with her baby, Joy?

What do you think of Claire's way of handling the meeting with Freddy? Did any of it surprise you?

What are your thoughts about Claire's suggestion to Freddy about self-forgiveness?

How do you feel about how Claire handled everything and about the 'deal' she offered Freddy? Did you think he would accept? If it had been up to you, would you have accepted? Why?

Chapter Eight Questions

What do you think about Freddy's name change to 'Abe'?

How do you feel when you get something done and know it was your effort that created the positive results? Can you share in Abe's feeling of getting the job at the car repair shop?

Are you surprised by how easily Claire gets along with everyone? How do you think she does it?

Have you ever helped someone transition to a new residence and living experience? If so, what was the experience like for you?

Do you think that Claire and Janine's real reason for asking for Abe's help was to be Piper's coach? How did you think it would work out?

What do you think of June's plan to have Doug tell the stories of each of his post cards to June and Gus? How do you suppose that made Doug feel?

Little Buddha Book Five

What do you think of the exchange between Abe and Mr. Rogers? Have you ever had an exchange like that? Were you made to apologize? If so, how did that feel?

Were you surprised that Abe learned from Claire and was able to legitimately apologize?

What do you think of Jax's chain analogy? How do you think it impacted Abe?

Do the links in the chain make sense to you? Do you think Abe will be able to use them effectively now? Could you use them too in difficult situations?

Chapter Nine Questions

Have you ever been around a lot of kids at once? Does it thrill you or overwhelm you? Do you feel like Claire, who loves the noise and excitement?

Did you like art when you were in school? Did you have an art teacher who encouraged you or did they expect you to follow all the rules?

Have you been around happy, excited children doing something they love and notice how they exemplify, 'joy'? What gives you joy?

Were you ever told that your coloring wasn't good enough, because you didn't stay within the lines? How did it make you feel? What do you think of how Claire interacted with Lucy?

Claire is very proud of her dad, Sam, for how he assists with his book study group. Would you like to be a part of it with him? What survival skill of yours would you talk about?

What are your thoughts about having a conversation with your 'self' and the five 'aspects' Sam discussed? Do you think it could work and shed some light for you?

Little Buddha Book Five

What are your thoughts about what Sam shared with the group? Can you see how his conversation changed his life and helped him take a new and better direction?

What are your thoughts about Dave's transformation experience?

Could you identify with Jamie's transformation experience of heaven? Did you sense a connection personally, even though it was Jamie's experience?

What do you think about Ranger's miracle transformation? Would you like your health to be transformed?

What sense did you get listening (reading) Dave's compassion transformation?

If you decided to experience a transformation, what 'profile' would you choose?

Chapter Ten Questions

Abe and Piper have been honest with each other about their mistakes. Is it hard for you to admit your mistakes to another person? If you do, how does it usually feel?

Were you surprised that Mr. Rogers was giving Abe a ride, given their first meeting went so badly?

Are there any friendships in your life that began from difficulties, like Abe and Mr. Rogers? If so, how did the friendship come about?

When Abe started telling Mr. Rogers the story about the man with two presents, what was your initial reaction? Did you feel you knew where the story was headed?

What would your reaction have been, to have sat next to the perfect stranger, then been offered one of two presents?

What are your thoughts about the story of the two presents and their contents? What does the note mean to you?

Little Buddha Book Five

Were you surprised that Sam allowed himself to be caught up in Maggie and Brad's argument?

Does Brad's childhood background shed light on his attitude about ownership for you? Did anything like this happen to you growing up?

Do you believe that Brad and Maggie can change their positions about gifts and ownership? If your opinions about ownership bother you for any reason, do you think you can change them?

How do you feel about Sam's shift from ownership to caretaking? Does it make sense to you?

Were you surprised that Claire took absolute control of things when Sam fainted?

What were your reactions to the birth of Brooke?

Little Buddha Book Five Notes

Little Buddha Book Five

Made in the USA
Middletown, DE
26 August 2023